Beans of Wisdom

7 Gifts for Great Leadership in
Business and Life

Joe Swinger

Beans of Wisdom

7 Gifts for Great Leadership in
Business and Life

LONDON   NUEVA YORK
MADRID   BARCELONA
MEXICO CITY   MONTERREY
BOGOTÁ   BUENOS AIRES

Published by
LID Publishing Inc.
420 Round Hill Rd. Greenwich,
Connecticut 06831, USA
Ph. +1 (203) 979 2964
contact@lidpublishing.com
LIDPUBLISHING.COM

A member of:

Printed in the USA

EAN-ISBN13: 9780985286439
Collection editor: Jeanne Bracken
Editing: Laurie Price
Typesetting: produccioneditorial.com
Cover design: ideas@nicandwill.com

First edition: February 2013

To Sandy,
who has showered me for many years
with her own Beans of Love

To Jonathan and Kevin,
the Coffee & Cocoa of my own life
and my two reasons for living on this Earth

Acknowledgments

There are many people to thank for helping make *Beans of Wisdom* a reality:

- My wife Sandy and sons Jonathan and Kevin, for their undying faith in both me and a project that seemed to take forever to manifest.

- LID Publishing and Marcelino Elosua for believing in this project from the very beginning.

- Raquel Avila, who is not only the best ally an author can have, but who is also a friend and confidante to whom I can vent to when necessary.

- Jeanne Bracken, for her skill at managing the entire editorial process and for exhibiting tolerance towards my never ending questions and input.

- Laurie Price for her excellent, insightful editing.

- Naike Hechem, for her passion and belief that this was a special project from the very beginning and one well worth undertaking.

- Cas Swinger, Elaine Rolke, John Swinger, Joanne Perone, Michael Swinger, Barbara Pondo, and John Johnston for offering their input and ideas on the concept and design of the book.

- George and Faye Nakamura for their continued support during the writing process.

- Casimir and Ruth Swinger for watching over my family while I oftentimes hid from them for weeks.

Joe Swinger, 2012

Contents

1

Encounter

You've probably lost something in the past. Maybe it was your car keys, your wallet or a credit card. If you're like me, the loss stays with you all day as you search your memory bank trying to remember when you had it last. You worry over it, sometimes becoming obsessed to the point that the anxiety totally ruins your day or week until you find the item. Sometimes you never find it.

It didn't hit me until this very minute, as I stood in a charitable food line on Christmas Eve, that I realized all I'd lost. Where did I go wrong? Why did I always seem to make wrong decisions at critical times? Why could I never show my true feelings?

I searched the full room of desperate people as I shuffled in the line. Unshaven men. Disheveled women. Unkempt kids. Did I really sink this low? I kept thinking it must be some big mistake.

"This can't be happening," I said to myself. "I'm better than this."

"I've been waiting for you."

I was jolted out of my stupor and turned to see a very large, old man dressed in a workman's shirt with the name Kris emblazoned on it. Kris – if that was his name – towered over the others as he stood ahead of me with a serving spoon in his hand.

"What?"

He motioned towards me with the serving spoon.

"Come on, Joe, I don't have all day," he said in a gruff voice. "It's Christmas Eve."

I stumbled forward to get the only food I'd eat on this day.

"How did you know my name was Joe," I asked.

"Like I said, I've been waiting for you."

I shuffled over with my tray to the only table that had any empty seats and joined a family of four. I politely nodded to a man that I presumed was the father. The two boys, a little younger than mine, chewed down the food like they hadn't eaten in days, and they probably hadn't.

I ate in silence, partially out of respect for those at my table and partially out of my fear to look up and let others see me.

I dipped my dinner roll in the gravy as it rolled off the turkey meat. God, I loved the holidays, especially when the family would gather around the dinner table laughing and singing Christmas songs. My wife would always be busy in the kitchen while I played with the boys in anticipation of the big meal.

Somehow, the turkey didn't taste the same now. I looked wistfully at the family across the table. The two boys, despite their surroundings, almost seemed to enjoy themselves. I wondered what their Christmas morning would look like.

"You have kids?"

The father's voice almost startled me.

"Two – twin six-year-old boys."

I could tell that the man was a little taken back by my having young boys at my advanced age.

"We got a late start."

The man nodded his head in acceptance. I continued to eat in silence, but then had a strong urge to continue our communication, though it was totally unlike me to talk to strangers.

"I was watching your boys. Looks like they're having a good time."

The man almost broke into a smile of pride as he rubbed the bigger boy's head.

"Yeah, we told them we're on a road trip. This here is Gabe. He's five. Billy just turned four. Twins, huh? Your boys have names?"

Why I hesitated for a moment I don't know, but I felt reluctant.

"Coffee and Cocoa."

I then got "that stare" that so often accompanies their names.

"Silly, right? It was my wife's idea."

"Those are some strange names, but colorful. Your favorite drinks, I suppose?"

"No, they were named after the color of their skin," I said apologetically. "We're a mixed family."

"Nothing wrong with that, I suppose. The world needs mixed families."

The man's wife stood up and began to collect the boys.

"We'd better get going, George."

George extended his hand. I paused for a second after noticing how filthy it was, but my manners got the best of me.

"It's been a pleasure, my friend. You enjoy this special day."

"Special day?" I asked.

"It's Christmas Eve. Something special always happens on Christmas Eve."

I played with my mashed potatoes and gravy for what seemed liked hours, but it probably only amounted to a few minutes. I wondered how George and his family ended up at this place. More importantly, how did they still seem so happy despite their circumstances?

My mind drifted as I wondered what my boys were doing this holiday, their first one without their dad. Would they sing Christmas songs with my wife around the table this evening?

"Mind if I join you?" the voice boomed.

It was Kris. He looked even bigger and more imposing on this side of the counter.

"Sure. I have nothing else going on and this food is terrible," I said as I pushed the plate away.

"That terrible food is all some people are going to eat today," Kris said in a reprimanding voice.

"Still, the management could probably do a better job if they wanted to. I'm sure they get some form of government money."

"You sound like you're a businessman, Joe. That true?"

I couldn't help but feel a touch of sarcasm in Kris' voice and, frankly, he was starting to bug me.

"Ivy League MBA, my friend," I bragged, smugly. "I owned one of the biggest restaurant chains in the state – seven locations that employed over 500 people at its height." I added proudly

"What happened? Don't tell me, the economy, right?" Kris remarked, sarcastically.

"Of course. What else?"

This guy really started to get my blood boiling. It was bad enough that I was eating lunch in a dump like this, but having some fat jerk question my business skills didn't sit well with me.

"I'll tell you what happened, smart guy. Have you ever run a business?"

I didn't even wait for an answer.

"All people heard about from the media was how bad businesses were having it, so customers started to think they had the upper hand. They began demanding discounts. They'd lie and say the food was bad so they wouldn't have to pay. And don't get me started on foreigners, they were the worst."

Kris nodded as if he understood, but I'm not sure he really did.

"And the employees. It was a constant round of hiring, training, and firing. You'd think that with such a terrible job market they'd want to keep their jobs, but that didn't seem to be the case. People nowadays just don't want to work. They'll quit over any little thing, like not getting a weekend off."

"Did you?" Kris shot back.

"Did I what?"

"Give them weekends off."

"When they deserved it, which wasn't very often."

"Maybe that would've made a difference," Kris offered, with a knowing smile.

"What was your excuse with the family?"

I asked myself why I was talking to this guy who obviously didn't understand where I was coming from.

"I'm sorry, friend, but have we met? You seem to think you know a lot about me and my situation."

"Forgive me, sometimes I can't help but interfere. Let's just say that I've been watching you for some time."

I jumped out of my chair thinking I was talking to some kind of stalker or perhaps someone hired by an irate business associate.

"It's been nice, Kris, but I'm outta here."

"Sit down!" Kris's voice boomed.

"Where are you going to go? Are you in a hurry to walk back to the shelter in this freezing weather?"

I slithered back down into my chair. Why, I don't know. Perhaps I was afraid that somehow Kris would go nuts on me and beat me to a pulp. More realistically, though, it was probably that he was right – I had no other place to go. I'd been living on the streets for weeks after I got evicted from my apartment for being unable to pay the rent and there was no change in sight.

Or – perhaps – in some fantasy world of mine buried deep within, I held out hope that Kris might have something to do with revealing the specialness of Christmas Eve – what George had told me about.

"Kris, you still here? Getting late, isn't it?"

The woman didn't have a name badge but, judging from the fact that she was young and Hispanic and there to clear the table, she must have been one of the kitchen employees.

"I'm just spending a little time here with my new friend, Joe."

"Oh, is he the lucky one? Good to meet you, Joe. I'm Monica, the manager of this soup kitchen."

I skeptically shook her hand and I seem to remember muttering hello.

"Joe doesn't like the food, Monica. He's used to owning fancy restaurants."

Monica turned one of one of the empty chairs around and plopped down on it.

"I think he wants to lodge a complaint," Kris continued.

"I'm sorry, Joe. We do the best we can here with the available resources. We're going to end up feeding 800 people today before we're through. But if you have any suggestions, I'm more than happy to hear them."

Why I froze at that moment, I don't know. Normally outspoken and ready with plenty of criticism, I found myself speechless. Perhaps I was still thinking about what Monica told me – about me being the lucky one. But lucky at what?

"Even better, I'd love it if you would volunteer here and lend us your management experience. I still have so much to learn and I'd like to know what you would do differently," Monica added with a smile.

"I'm sorry, but I'm in no condition to do that now. Maybe when times are better," I said as my voice trailed off.

"It's time to go, Joe," Kris remarked as he quickly rose from his chair.

"Go? Go where?" I answered incredulously.

"We have to hurry – it's getting late. I have a limo waiting outside for us."

Limo? I just got done eating a terrible meal at a soup kitchen and now I'm going to be driven back to the shelter in a limo? This *was* a special day, indeed.

2 | Invitation

The limo was a stretch. This guy must be some important businessman, I surmised. Probably makes him feel good to take pity on someone who's lost everything.

I stepped into the limo and paused to admire how spacious the interior was. I settled into the leather seats and grabbed the bottled water that Kris handed me.

I had to chuckle as I visualized the view to someone on the outside peering in – seeing this bum in tattered clothes sitting inside.

"What do you think?" Kris asked.

"I'll tell you what I think," I asserted, deliberately.

"I think you're some rich big shot who's getting a kick out of giving a ride to some homeless bum on a cold Christmas Eve."

"You think that's what all of this is about?"

"Hell yes, that's what I think! I saw guys like you when I was in the restaurant business. You spend a few hours volunteering like you really give a crap and then you go home to your 5,000-square-foot house feeling smug like you made someone's holiday."

Finally! I had my attitude back – I was on a roll.

"That's not the worst of it. Then you go to your rich country club where you tell all your idiot friends how you partied like a rock star with a few bums over the holidays and, hopefully, generated some good karma."

"Let's go – we're late enough."

The limo driver started the car on Kris' command and pulled away from the curb. Suddenly, he pulled a hard u-turn – is that even possible in a limo, I wondered – and we began heading north.

"What's going on? The shelter is back the other way."

"Who said we were going to the shelter, Joe?"

I began to panic. So, there *was* an associate behind all of this and I *was* being kidnapped. I looked around the limo for – I don't know what – something to hit Kris over the head with?

"Am I being kidnapped? Did someone hire you to kill me and dump my body out in the boonies?"

As crazy as I wanted to believe the idea sounded, the reality was that I probably deserved what I was about to get.

Kris chuckled.

"Sit down, Joe. We have a ways to go."

Kris and I sat in silence as the limo drove through neighborhoods I never knew existed and past areas I'd never want to step foot in.

"The truth is that I was in a similar place as you not so long ago," Kris disclosed as he stared out the window for several moments, maybe reminiscing about where he'd come from.

"I'm giving back just like I promised I would."

We drove again in silence for what seemed to be a considerable amount of time. Judging by the sun's position, I guessed it was around 1pm. Since I no longer owned a watch, I couldn't be sure.

I remembered back to when I'd pawned my Rolex – how many times did I still look at my wrist for the time? I'd always gotten a kick out of wearing a stylish watch since all of the worker bees used their cell phones to tell the time.

I looked at my wrist where the shiny Rolex had always been and couldn't help notice that the scar was healing nicely.

"What did you mean about giving back?" I finally had to ask.

I must have asked a sensitive question since Kris didn't have a ready answer and was peering out the window. I also noticed that the limo had left the city folk behind and was speeding past a country landscape.

Kris used the occasion to stare me solemnly and squarely in the eyes. It was kind of weird, actually, to see him grasping for words.

"What if you had an opportunity to receive some of the greatest gifts in the world? To have the most amazing secrets revealed to you – what would you dare ask for?"

I quickly thought that I would ask for a pile of cash and get the hell out of my situation, but somehow I knew that money wasn't going to be a part of the equation.

Now Kris was on a roll.

"Gifts that would guarantee your success? Your happiness? Maybe, more importantly, other people's success and happiness?"

I didn't answer right away for fear of making a fool of myself. One nice thing about being a business owner is that you're never wrong and everyone else is never right. No one would ever question my decisions – my leadership – so it was easy to be the one with all the answers.

Not until that very instant did it occur to me that *that* could have been my problem.

I hate to admit it, but Kris was starting to get my attention. It sounded like a bunch of hooey, but maybe there was more to this limo ride than a warm leather seat to the shelter. At least I started to hope so. That's what living on the street will do to a man.

"Alright, Kris. You've piqued my interest. What's going on?"

Kris turned with a look in his eyes that I have only seen a few times in my life – a look that spoke volumes about the power of what he was about to reveal – to me.

"Have you ever heard of the Beans of Wisdom?"

I hadn't, and something told me it wasn't ever served in one of my restaurants, either.

"Is that why we're driving all this way – to pick up some beans?"

Kris flipped me an incredulous look.

"The Beans are the greatest, life empowering attributes we've received from the Source, to experience life. Their power lies in the fact that they truly are the only antidote to our mechanical ways of thinking that fight to destroy life here on Earth."

"Tell me more," I begged.

"Centuries ago, there was a secret organization that performed a ritual every Christmas Eve. Parents from all across the town brought their young children to receive those gifts of remembrance from the masters of the day in order to become productive citizens in society."

Kris paused for a moment, to build the suspense.

"Some years ago, a wise man – fed up with the way the world had changed and with people's cynicism and hatred – began the ritual again."

Kris let the story hang at that point, as if I would understand – but I didn't.

"That's a great story, Kris, but it might as well be a fairy tale – I'm not a kid anymore. What's it got to do with me now – I'm living on the streets?"

"One adult per year. That's who gets an opportunity to have the secrets revealed to them and receive the same gifts that changed my life and those of countless others."

"No offense – but if you're offering me the opportunity to participate – and I think you are – it's a little late for an antidote in my life, isn't it? You think I'm just going to eat some beans and suddenly get my life back? My family?"

"Yes, that's exactly what I mean."

We drove in silence as I aimlessly gazed out the limo window. A thousand thoughts raced through my head as the barren landscape whizzed by.

Did Kris have some kind of magic bean or was I destined to live my life forever homeless? And, even if such a bean existed, why would I be the recipient?

A sudden dangerous feeling began to stir – a feeling I'd experienced many times while my life was falling apart. A feeling of hope.

How many times had hope let me down in the past? How many times did I hope that I wouldn't lose my business – my home – my family?

"There it is," Kris piped up, breaking the silence.

I saw it – out in the distance – a small house rising from the middle of nowhere.

"It's time for your decision, Joe. I'm offering you an opportunity to be a part of something that you'll only get one chance at in a lifetime."

"I don't even have a clue about what I'd be doing. Would I be giving out some beans to a bunch of kids?"

"Yeah, something like that."

"What's it going to cost me? I know there has to be a catch, right?"

"Of course, there's a catch. All opportunities come with a cost – didn't you learn that at your Ivy League school? I told you – I've been watching you – this wasn't an impulsive decision. I chose you."

"I still don't understand. Why me? If these beans are so great, why get a homeless person when you can get anyone you want?"

"There's no more time for questions, Joe. Either you commit – right now – to be fully in and honor the promise you must make of giving back for the rest of your working life or I'll have the limo drive you back to the shelter and there's no hard feelings."

I quickly racked my brain with all the permutations of my circumstances as the once distant house now loomed larger ahead. It occurred to me that it was really a no-brainer. What if I just agreed to give back, but didn't actually do it? How would Kris even know?

"What will it be?" Kris demanded.

"I'm in," I pronounced, arrogantly.

The limo turned right onto the street. I scanned the area for a street sign that would tell me where I was, but came up empty. And then I saw it – lying on the ground alongside a signpost was a rusty, mangled piece of metal with the words Wisdom Lane.

3

Purple

Here was one of the strangest sights I'd ever seen – a huge structure – was it a farmhouse – out in the middle of nowhere with one small road leading to it and nothing else around. The "neighborhood" looked as if it had been built for one reason and one reason only. There were a few bare trees like nothing more than some large twigs scattered along the street in the winter air.

The limo passed the structure, which up close, had an almost renaissance look and feel to it, and then we parked in the back.

"This is where I bid you goodbye, my friend," Kris said abruptly as he began to step out of the limo.

"Wait a minute! What happens to me?" I demanded.

"You'll be given instructions on how to move forward. Good luck."

Kris began to shut the door, but then stopped and opened it wide enough to poke his head in.

"I'm glad you stayed, Joe. I know you'll discover that we both made the right decision."

Kris was off and the limo made another one of its unforgettable u-turns and retraced the path we had just driven, pulling alongside what I assumed was the front of the building.

"We'll wait here for five minutes."

The limo driver spoke with an accent, though I couldn't place its origin.

"Gotta name?" I asked.

"The name is Jerry, Boss."

Jerry was one of those drivers who likes to talk to you while looking in his rear view mirror rather than turn around and speak face to face.

"Well, Jerry, maybe *you* can tell me what the hell is going on?"

"Nothin' goin' on, Boss. Just good fun for the kids. You'll see."

I looked around and saw nothing that might resemble good fun – not today or any day.

"Well, Jerry, maybe you haven't noticed because you've been driving, but we're out in the middle of nowhere and there isn't a kid in sight. Doesn't that make you wonder?"

"No, Boss. You'll see – it's like magic. The entire street will be lined with kids and lights."

Even though it bugged me at first that Jerry called me Boss, there was a certain likeability about him. He seemed to have – what was it – a type of contentment that made me believe him. Or was that my hope springing up again?

Jerry peered into his mirror and gave his best impression of looking me in the eyes.

"It's time, Boss. Don't worry – just let it happen."

I received Jerry's instructions and got ready to go when he startled me by turning around to face me.

"See you on the other side, Boss," he smiled.

I couldn't help but think about what Jerry had just said as I walked towards the house – about seeing me on the other side. The other side of what?

I paused in front of the entrance – doubt and indecision in my mind. Again, I asked myself the question – why me? What did Kris see in me that made him believe I had something to contribute?

Believe. The word stuck in my head. What exactly *did* I believe in? How did I reach a point in my life where others believed in me more than I did? I used to be unstoppable.

I hesitantly entered the building as instructed and was enveloped in complete darkness. A musty smell filled the air, as if the house had been sitting vacant for a long time. There was also a faint smell of – was that paint?

Jerry was very specific about where I was to go – the purple room – even though it didn't make any sense. I crept forward down the dark passageway half expecting some Halloween creature to jump out at me. This place was for kids I asked myself?

The darkness was disorienting to the point where I didn't know if I was going to bump into an obstacle – or worse – step into some kind of trap door. A brief panic ran down my spine.

It was impossible to find a door, let alone a name on one. Then I saw it – a faint glow of light ahead that appeared out of nowhere like magic – and I immediately assumed that it came from under the door. I approached it with caution and nervously felt the door with my hands.

Purple – this was it! I knocked twice on the door, just as Jerry instructed me to do. I hate to admit it, but my heart began to pound with anticipation. Even though the whole thing seemed strange, it was much more exciting than sitting in the homeless shelter.

The door slowly opened and there on the other side was – Kris? What the heck was *he* doing there?

"I've been waiting for you," he said with a smile.

The room was small, windowless and awash in dull light from above. The walls – an antiseptic white – were bare and matched the rest of the room. A ladder leaned conspicuously against a small table with dozens of small, purple boxes on it and a matching mirror on the wall behind it. And then there was still that paint smell.

"It's good to see you again, Joe. You've come very far in such a short time."

"It's good to see you again too, Kris. What's it been, like 10 minutes? I need to know – now – why you brought me here."

"Why – to paint, of course."

Kris opened a closet door and out came an opened can of purple paint, as well as some brushes and a roller.

"You're joking, right?"

"No joke. We can't have a purple room with white walls now, can we?"

I remembered what Jerry had said about not worrying and just letting it happen. I grabbed the ladder without another word and went to work.

I finished the last brush stroke and stepped back to admire my work. Not bad for a homeless guy! I returned the room to its previous arrangement and carefully pushed the small table back against the wall.

"What's in the boxes, Kris?"

At that moment, I sensed Kris's powerful presence as he walked up from behind although he had been inside the room the entire time.

I gingerly picked up one of the boxes and examined it. It was about the size of a ring case, very plainly wrapped; it appeared to hold no real significance.

"One of the Beans?" I asked.

Kris answered with silence.

I put the box back on the table.

"Where do they come from? I mean, who makes them and puts all of this together?"

"Suffice it to say that the Beans are naturally and organically created with input from the greatest minds – both past and present. The rest you'll discover as we go along."

With both his hands, Kris picked up the box and extended it toward me.

"Your antidote, Joe."

My heart raced as I took the box, slowly opened it, and peered at its contents for several seconds. Inside was a uniquely shaped and carefully placed purple Bean. I chewed the Bean for several seconds with my eyes shut so that I could truly savor its flavor – and power.

"What do you feel?" Kris whispered.

"It tastes like..."

"*Not* taste. Feel. What do you feel?"

The truth was that I was feeling many things when I opened my eyes and suddenly caught a glimpse of my reflection in the mirror. I moved in for a closer look and fixated on the sight for the longest time – because I just didn't recognize the individual staring back at me. Was it the dull light, or something else?

For the first time I saw who I truly was and what I had become.

"I feel as if I don't know why I'm here. That I don't recognize that man in the mirror," I muttered.

Kris grabbed the paintbrush that was sitting off to the side and held it up for me to see.

"Why is this here?"

"I'm not sure I get you, Kris."

"What is the reason for this brush being here – at this moment?"

It sounded like a ridiculous question at the time, but I answered it anyway.

"To paint the walls, of course."

"Of course," Kris confirmed.

Then Kris pointed to the ladder.

"Why is this ladder here?"

"To help reach the tops of the walls. Where are you going with this?" I begged.

"The paintbrush has a purpose. The ladder has a purpose. What is *your* purpose, Joe?"

I was stunned by the question, and the more I thought about it the more speechless I became. What *was* my purpose?

"I don't know, Kris. I don't know if I've ever known."

Kris bent down to pick something off the floor – a mousetrap – and waved it in front of me.

"Even a mousetrap has a purpose, Joe. Aren't you more important than a mousetrap?"

"The first Bean of Wisdom is the Purple Bean of Purpose. Life without a purpose – is no life at all. Everything comes from purpose – our passions, our confidence, our creativity and our dreams."

Kris was on a roll – again.

"You live your life in doubt, fearful and disoriented – just as you did when you entered this building for the first time. Stumbling in the dark like a blind person hoping that someone – anyone – will turn a light on for you to help you find your way."

"*You* need to become that light, Joe – for others who are stumbling just as you were. You must listen to your inner voice and what it's telling you."

"You see, in order to be a great leader, you must first truly know your own purpose before you can help others find theirs. How else can you help your employees who are stumbling in their own darkness? This then earns you the right to mentor others, whether they are your employees or your loved ones."

I stood in silent agony. How could I not – everything Kris said was completely true. I began to think back to my restaurant days and how I treated my employees. I thought I'd offered them support and guidance, but I didn't. It was always about me and how much money I made. How many employees did I lose because they were stumbling in the dark and failing just because I wasn't able to show them the light and help them succeed?

"The paintbrush – the ladder – the mousetrap. None of those items know their true purpose – they just exist until we act upon them and show them their true purpose, and that allows them to offer their true beauty."

"It's the same with your employees – your loved ones – even your enemies. Help them find their true purpose and *your* business will skyrocket, *your* loved ones will blossom, and *your* enemies will become your allies."

Kris was passionate and spellbinding – and he was right. Me – a mentor? How I would love to know what my purpose in life was so that I'd be able to guide others like he envisioned I could. But how was I to find it?

"The first Bean of Wisdom is the Bean of Purpose. Everything comes from purpose – our passions, our confidence, our creativity and our dreams."

4

Red

Have you ever had your identity – who you thought you were – ripped from you in such a way that you lost all sense of who you were? Maybe you were blindsided by a divorce or terminated from a job, whereby who you were and the life you were living immediately changed?

Several minutes before, I knew who I was – a homeless bum on the streets – but at least it was an identity. Now, I wasn't sure who I'd become. It was as if the Joe I knew had become an anonymous life form, ready to be shaped like a handful of Play-Doh.

I thought back to how long I'd gone through life seemingly sure of my purpose. My years spent in college and my dreams of how I was going to do great things – and possibly change the world – and do so profitably. Did I choose the wrong path – or was my path changing before my very eyes?

I was still dazed by the experience I'd just been through when Kris told me it was time to move on. I silently asked myself 'how much more can I take?' Was it even safe to go any further, I wondered?

I opened the door and prepared to leave. I looked into Kris' eyes and we exchanged an unspoken acknowledgement to go forward.

I'm ashamed to admit that – for the briefest second – I wanted to hug the man that I'd just met a short time ago. However, I'm even more ashamed to admit that I regretted not doing it as soon as the door shut behind me.

Kris instructed me to go to the red door – that was next door – and give it the requisite two knocks. The hallway was still dark and I couldn't help but wonder about what the kids – if any – were going to do if they actually did come for the Beans.

Out of the silence jumped a murmur that was difficult to place. Was something going on outside? I couldn't pay much attention to it since I'd already arrived at the red door.

Once again my heart began to race, but in a different way than before. This time I wondered what great episode waited for me on the other side, as well as who would be behind the door, since I was absolutely certain it couldn't be Kris.

The door opened to a warm red glow and the silhouette of a female figure. It took my eyes a second to adjust to the light, but there was no doubt who the woman was.

"Monica!" I blurted, excitedly.

Yes, it was Monica – no longer in her soup kitchen garb, but wearing a red holiday dress. She reached out her arms for a hug and, unlike the reticence I felt with Kris, I immediately jumped into them as if I had found an old friend. Perhaps I had.

"What are *you* doing here? I thought you were at the soup kitchen."

"I'm giving back as I promised I would. The kitchen is in fine hands for the rest of the day."

I hesitantly entered the room and immersed myself in the red light's glow.

Monica gave the room a wave.

"What do you think? Pretty cool, huh?"

I was speechless as I looked up at what appeared to be a celestial event above my head. Dozens of miniature red mobiles hung from the ceiling throughout the room. The different shapes were incredible – stop signs, fire hydrants, tomatoes, peppers, strawberries, cherries, raspberries, fire engines, stop-lights, the planet Mars and The Great Red Spot of Jupiter.

The room was arranged in an entirely different manner than the Purple room. The walls were red, of course, but there was an odd assortment of small tables scattered about with empty vases on them. And – as in the Purple room – a ladder leaned against a small table that held dozens of small boxes on it and a matching mirror – but this time the boxes were red.

However, the most conspicuous piece in the room was a framed, acrylic display sitting on a table full of beautiful, red butterflies – lots of them.

"I just love the color red, don't you, Joe?"

"I guess green has always been my favorite color – you know, money."

I don't know what it was, but seeing Monica here gave me a completely different impression of her. I almost felt embarrassed about what I'd thought about her at the soup kitchen.

"Have you ever asked yourself why so many things in life are red?"

"No, I never gave it much thought." I uttered.

"And not just things, but emotions, too – guilt, passion, anger, rage – love, sex. Perhaps it's because red is the longest wavelength discernible by the human eye?"

Monica moved closer to me in a way that became uncomfortable.

"You know what I would like you to do, Joe?"

I didn't, and even if I did, I was too paralyzed by Monica's beauty to speak.

"I want you to fill this room up with love!"

"Excuse me?"

"Why do you think that all things concerning love are the color red, Joe?"

Yeah – I pretty much just stood there, mute, like an idiot.

"Didn't your Ivy League school teach you anything about love?" Monica grinned. "I suppose not, huh?"

Monica produced a bunch of decorative heart mobiles and fanned them out in her hands.

"Is it because our hearts are red? Our blood?"

Monica handed me the hearts and instructed me to get on the ladder – and hang them from the ceiling interspersed among all the other mobiles. So yes, up the ladder I went, to mingle amongst the vegetables, fruits and planets and spread my love around the room – and the solar system – as I had never done before.

I wish I could describe the incredible feeling I had when I came down the ladder, looked up at the ceiling and saw the mobiles ripple as if they were a red sea of love, but words would not do it justice. It was something I'd never quite experienced before – such calmness, such warmth – and it was something I'd helped create.

Monica put her hand on my shoulder and shared the hushed moment before leaning in towards me.

"We have to hurry," she breathed into my ear.

I was amazed by the way I was shuffled around, first by Kris, and now Monica, as if we were on some kind of important time schedule. Perhaps we were.

Monica edged towards the butterfly display, circling it like a tiger its prey.

"Beautiful aren't they? They're called Crimson Callicore – from South America – probably the brightest red butterflies in the world."

I peered inside the case for several moments. There were several spectacular looking red butterflies inside; I had never seen this kind before. It was amazing how they retained their beauty, even though they were no longer alive.

There were also several caterpillars in different stages of development on the base of the display. As I stared at them, it occurred to me that it was like seeing the recent stages of my life.

I was in the egg stage – emotionally isolated – for the majority of my existence. I was the crawling caterpillar, homeless and scrounging around on the ground for something to eat in the hopes of just surviving another day.

"The butterfly has an interesting life cycle, no?" Monica said.

"Yes, I was just thinking about it. The Chrysalis –"

"That's where all the action takes place," Monica stated as she finished my sentence. "The metamorphosis. Amazing, isn't it, how one ugly creature can enter the pupa and another beautiful creature emerges."

Monica cupped my face with her hands and looked into my confused eyes.

"I believe there's a beautiful creature inside of each of us, don't you Joe?"

I stood speechless as I admired the beauty and awareness in Monica's eyes.

"There's a proverb that says 'just when the caterpillar thought the world was over, it became a butterfly.' Tell me about your world, Joe. Like the caterpillar, did you think it was over?"

I wish I could say that I was able to give her an articulate answer, but I would be lying. The truth is, unlike the caterpillar, I understood what was happening. I understood that I was losing my family, business and home.

End of the world? It was *more* than that. I don't believe a caterpillar contemplates or attempts to end it all as I did, although I was such a loser that I even failed at that.

Monica led me to a large box on the floor that was upright in the corner of the room. Inside were several long-stemmed roses and she instructed me to put them in the vases.

I reached into the box to grab a bunch and shrieked when I came away with a handful of thorns. I yelled to Monica for a pair of gloves so that I could finish the job.

"Gloves?"

"Yes, my hands got stabbed by all the thorns!" I screamed.

"First of all, they're called prickles, not thorns," Monica reprimanded as she picked up one of the roses I'd dropped.

"Second, this rose is not meant to be handled like a piece of meat. Each stem has its own beauty, its own elegance."

Monica held the rose as if it were a newborn baby, gently caressing its petals before she put it into a vase.

"This vase will be the rose's home for the rest of its life. Its beauty and fragrance can only be enjoyed for a short time. That's not something to take lightly."

Monica took me by the hand to the table with the red boxes and stood me in front of the mirror. I stood in silence for several moments until Monica came up from behind and gently touched my shoulder. She picked up a box with two hands and extended it toward me.

"For *your* metamorphosis, Joe"

My heart raced again, just as it had done in the purple room, but this time with a jolt of anticipation as I wondered what great gift I was about to receive.

I slowly opened the box and again, peered at the contents for several seconds. This time, inside was a uniquely shaped and carefully placed red Bean. I chewed the Bean, like before, for several seconds with my eyes shut so that I could truly savor its flavor – and its power.

"What do you feel?" Monica asked.

I'm embarrassed to say that before I could even open my eyes, I began to tremble and tears were streaming down my cheeks. My reaction to the Bean was so powerful and overwhelming that it confused me, momentarily, as to what was happening.

I opened my eyes and again saw my reflection in the mirror. But, unlike the last time, when I didn't recognize myself, this time it was very different and very emotional. I wasn't quite sure what I felt, because – I don't know – perhaps I'd never felt this emotion before.

The man in the mirror – whom I had spent years berating and cursing and calling all sorts of names for his failures in life – was looking back at me with only one expectation.

"I just want to be loved," I muttered, as tears rolled down my face.

"The second Bean of Wisdom is the Red Bean of Love. Life without love – is no life at all. Everything we have to offer and give to others comes from love – our caring, our time, our talents and our desire to make another person feel happy and special."

This time it was Monica who was on a roll.

"You want to be loved just as the butterfly wants to be loved. Just as the rose wants to be loved. The ability to love is one of our greatest gifts in the world. You live your life feeling miserable because you think you're a failure or you're not doing what you think you should be doing. The truth is, you are doing exactly what you should be doing at this moment."

"Your employees are like caterpillars waiting to blossom into butterflies. As a great leader, you must help to facilitate their metamorphoses in ways they're not aware of. But, to be able to do this, you must learn to love yourself before you can truly love another."

Monica again led me to the area where the roses lay on the floor.

"Look at this rose as if it were an employee," Monica exclaimed as she held it up to my face. "Some appear to be filled with nothing but prickles and are difficult to get along with. However, if you look closely, you'll see that they also have their own beauty, their own fragrance. This is the part you must cultivate – to let their inner beauty shine in their own unique ways."

I finished putting the remainder of the roses into the vases, picking them up one by one and admiring them in their entirety – their prickles and their flowers – while all the time wondering if I were truly capable of accepting another individual for what they were – flaws and all.

More importantly, I wondered how I'd ever be able to accept myself, unconditionally. How long would I be in my own stage of metamorphosis and, like the caterpillar, would a beautiful butterfly finally emerge?

"The second Bean of Wisdom is the Bean of Love. Everything we have to offer and give to others comes from love – our caring, our time, our talents and our desire to make another person feel happy and special."

5

Rainbow

Love is a strange thing. We go through life believing we love others, and often even telling them so without thinking twice about it. But, do we *really* love them? Unconditionally, with no strings attached? Or, is it just a word that rolls off of our tongues easily after many years?

I thought about the way I'd treated my family. Did I truly express my love or was I just saying the words? Was it a surprise that my wife left me? Despite the loss of my business and home, was it reasonable to assume she'd stick beside me, or had I deluded myself into thinking I was loved in return? Was I as selfish as she said I was, putting my dreams – my business – ahead of my family?

How many employees did I terminate because I didn't empathize with what they were feeling or going through in their lives? How could I have truly cared about them if I failed to give them time off they needed to spend with their family or friends?

The thoughts jolted out of my head as Monica briefed me on where to go next, which was the Rainbow room at the end of the hall. I left the red room after hugging her goodbye and thanking her for the moments she'd shared with me.

I stepped out into the hallway, which was plunged into darkness as the red door closed behind me. Again, I heard sounds emanating from outside, just as I had the last time I'd stood there, though this time they seemed much louder than before.

Then I noticed a bluish light that broke the stillness of what appeared to be the end of the hallway. Curious, I carefully made my way down to it and, as I did, the sounds grew in intensity.

The bluish light – and the sounds – were indeed coming from the rainbow room since the door was ajar. I knocked twice nonetheless, but received no answer. Conjuring up a bit of audacity, I entered the room, not knowing what to expect.

The room, lit up by winter sun through uncovered windows, was laid out similarly to the other rooms. Yes – there was another ladder – as well as a table with boxes on it – that I presumed were the Beans. However, at that moment I was more interested in what was going on outside than what the room looked like.

I inched closer to the windows to peek. What I discovered was something I wouldn't have believed just a short time ago.

Workers – dozens of them – were decorating the trees with Christmas lights. Others appeared to be preparing the street for some kind of event. After observing for several moments, I found myself asking a dangerous question – could this really be happening? Are kids *really* going to come here for the magic Beans?

"What do you think?"

I just about hit the ceiling when I heard the voice behind my right shoulder. I quickly turned around and, undoubtedly, wore a look of terror. For the first time during the entire day, I experienced real fear. Not the kind of fear I'd already felt – of the unknown – but this time, of being in danger.

"My name is Singh. Good to meet you, Joe."

Singh was everything that I resented in my business – and life. I couldn't tell you what ethnic group he came from, but that wouldn't matter. Suffice it to say, he wore a turban on his head and spoke with an accent – and you can probably guess the rest.

Singh was also the first stranger I encountered in the building, so far, and it definitely lent itself to a bad feeling. I probably made matters worse by refusing to shake the man's hand.

"Hello," I said stiffly. "What's a guy like *you* doing here?"

"You mean someone wearing a turban?" Singh chuckled. "My dear friend, you think people like you are the only ones to celebrate Christmas? Christmas is a state of mind. It's a way of living, 365 days a year. My sons may not have the Santa Claus *your* sons have or the Christmas tree *your* sons have, but I can assure you that the spirit definitely lives inside my boys."

Singh turned towards me with what appeared to be an evil eye.

"Can you say the same?"

Of course, it was a question I couldn't answer in the affirmative.

"Look at that," Singh remarked as he gazed out the window alongside me. "It's amazing what people can accomplish when they work together."

"Yeah, all we need is snow to make it a perfect day," I added sarcastically.

"Of course there'll be snow – that isn't a question," Singh chastised. "The higher power never lets the children down."

"Have you ever thought of how many races, religions, and ethnicities there are in the world?" Singh continued. "It is pretty remarkable that we get along."

"That's just it – we don't," I shot back. "You should know that better than anyone."

"Sounds like you have a little anger in you, my friend."

"Anger? How about rage?" I vehemently went off on Singh. "Constantly complaining about my food? Cutting prices to put me out of business? Not only did you wreck my life, you are wrecking the entire country."

"I wrecked your life *and* the country? I didn't know I was so powerful!" Singh mocked.

"You know what I mean."

"Oh, you mean people like me – people who are different. You mean because I wear a turban I am one of *those people* who go around creating trouble for everyone, correct?"

"My friend, you went out of business because you failed as a business owner – no other reason," Singh coldly preached. "As far as your country, well – I would look to your leaders for that one. However, we will deal with your anger later. But, for now, we have work to do."

"Yeah, I figured that when I saw the ladder," I added sadly.

I suddenly understood why the hallway was dark all this time. It was waiting for me to come along and hang up the Christmas lights!

Singh guided me to boxes – totes really – that were stacked in a corner of the room. He instructed me to empty each one to prepare for hanging the lights and putting up the Christmas tree.

One by one I opened the totes – while my eyes teared up – I was overcome with emotion. Memories of putting up my own Christmas tree and lights with my family – with my little boys – flooded my head.

I wondered how the tree looked this year and just how much joy I was missing? Who hung the Christmas lights – was there another man? I wondered how many gifts – if any – were under the tree and how excited my boys would be.

I encountered many items that I normally wouldn't call ornaments – in my world at least. Old children's shoes, small candles, pieces of straw, shafts of wheat and little gnome statues.

The lights were the traditional string ones that I was accustomed to, although these were multi-colored lights rather than the all white ones I'd hung at home.

The room became aglow when Singh turned on the overhead hallway lights so we could work. It's amazing what light – or awareness – can do to one's perception. The first place that I'd encountered when entering the building – that had me deathly afraid because of the unknown – was no longer a threat at all, and now appeared to be no more than just a long hallway one might find in a public school.

There was also an alcove with a mirror near the front door. I later learned that it would house the Christmas tree, to welcome the children as they arrived.

I stepped onto the ladder and began to hang the lights as instructed – and something amazing happened that hadn't happened for as long as I could remember – I found myself whistling as I worked. I smiled when I realized it; even though I was now homeless, I could once again enjoy the Christmas season.

Singh plunged the hallway into darkness by turning off the overhead lights. Within seconds, however, the Christmas lights switched on and illuminated the hallway with a beautiful, festive feeling. It was amazing – dozens of colored strands of light danced above my head.

For one bright moment, as I lost myself in the vivid, heavenly delight, I could have been the richest man anywhere in the world.

Singh stood near me under the lights and admired the work.

"You did a very nice job, my friend. Now, let's see what you can do with the Christmas tree. You'll find the body and the branches near the alcove where you should build it."

When I reached the alcove I knew something was wrong. It was the most ridiculous thing – there was no tree – there were no branches. Instead I discovered a pile of stainless steel rods and what looked to be like – shelves?

"Singh – what gives? This looks like it's meant for an office supply store."

Singh sighed and reluctantly made his way to the alcove where he slapped the rods together in an abrupt manner. Soon he had the tree looking like a giant tripod and he quickly placed the shelves into it.

"Obviously, you've done this before."

Singh had trouble snapping a few of the shelves in place, but finally did so after a brief struggle.

"There – now all you have to do is put the ornaments and decorations on the shelves."

"That's a Christmas tree?" I questioned in disbelief. "It looks like something one would use as a plant holder."

"Yes, it's a Christmas tree – just not *your* definition of a Christmas tree."

I decorated the "tree" as directed and stepped back to admire my work, which actually didn't look too bad. There were six shelves, including the one at the very top. The ornaments that had looked so strange when taken out of the totes really didn't seem out of place on the shelves. In fact, I kind of liked the look!

I bent down to pick up the remaining ornaments that didn't fit on the tree and caught my reflection in the mirror as I stood back up.

It was then that I saw Singh standing behind me. This made me feel uneasy even though I knew he represented no danger.

"For your cleansing, Joe" he nearly whispered as he handed me the rainbow colored box.

I deliberately chewed the rainbow colored Bean that I found inside the box. I noticed I was much calmer this time, maybe because I'd already been through the process twice before.

"What do you feel?" Singh asked.

I didn't answer Singh right away because I couldn't articulate what I felt in that moment, though I was sure I'd never felt it before. My body began to tremble and it seemed that my involuntary nervous system was losing control.

I opened my eyes, looked into the mirror and was stunned by what I saw. I stretched out my arms – like in the famous Da Vinci drawing of the Vitruvian Man. I felt a radiance that I'd never before experienced. I saw myself like a human prism, my body cast off a spectrum of light as the Christmas lights behind me seemed to shoot from my body. I know this sounds crazy – but it was as if all of the negative energy was draining from me – leaving an empty void to fill with goodness and purpose.

"I just want acceptance."

"The third Bean of Wisdom is the Rainbow Bean of Tolerance. Life without tolerance – is no life at all. Everything that allows us to function in the world with others comes from tolerance – our acceptance of others' opinions, the way we value our differences and the patience we show for our loved ones."

"But maybe even more important is acceptance of and tolerance for ourselves – for our own failures and shortcomings. It's impossible to hear your own inner voice if you're continually filled with anger – or rage."

"Look at this Christmas tree," Singh pointed out. "You saw it as nothing more than a plant holder, but another person sees it for its beauty – as a representation of their holiday's greater meaning. The straw and wheat ornaments that you saw as ridiculous, another sees as sacred – even as symbols of abundance and prosperity."

"Look at the lights above. Notice how the blue works with the green, and the green works with the red and the red works with the white. Each bulb – each color – is important to the overall effect of its beauty."

I stood mesmerized as Singh spoke. It was hard not to admire him since his words were so passionate – and so wise.

"As a great leader you have to remember that *everyone* is important," Singh continued. "Your subordinate wants to shine, just like that blue light. Your superior wants to shine, just like that green light. Your loved ones want to shine, just like that red light. No matter what race, color, creed, age or sex."

"No child enters this world without tolerance. You didn't enter this world fearing men wearing turbans," Singh lectured. "It is man who causes our difficulty to practice tolerance – because of our conditioning. We learn to hate certain groups or people based on what they said or did, or on how we were raised."

I went off into the Rainbow room to finish putting away the totes and reflect on what I'd just experienced. Everything suddenly seemed so clear that it puzzled me why I hadn't originally thought like this. Did my restaurants fail because I was a bad businessman as Singh said? Did my own beliefs doom me to failure?

I wondered how things might have been had I always hired the best job candidate rather than allowing my prejudices to cloud my judgment. How many good people did I turn down that might've made a difference? How many of my employees never offered a brilliant idea because they knew I would never listen to it?

It made me feel somber to realize that I was the one responsible for the results of my life, and that I had been the one sabotaging myself. However, it was also liberating – because if I was honestly responsible for those negative results, then I was also empowered to create results that were more positive, and that was a thought I could embrace.

"The third Bean of Wisdom is the Bean of Tolerance. Everything that allows us to function in the world with others comes from tolerance – our acceptance of others' opinions, the way we value our differences and the patience we show for our loved ones."

6

White

I knew immediately upon meeting Singh that he was one of those people I'd never forget. Maybe it was because he was close to my own age; in any case, he had such a clear perspective about life and he was someone you just don't encounter every day. It made me to wonder how many other people I meet and frivolously dismiss, thinking they're of no use to me, and even seeing them as a source of displeasure.

I wondered – what if each person we met in our daily lives had the potential to offer us some extraordinary gift or insight into ourselves? Imagine the impact and the direction our lives might take. Maybe this is the real definition behind serendipity.

It pains me to say this, but I realized that even I didn't have tolerance for my own two sons' ethnic background, and that I'd viewed it as a personal source of embarrassment over the last six years. Not only were their names hard for me to accept, but the necessity of having to explain to everyone I met that my boys were of mixed descent always made me feel uncomfortable. How I wished I could be given another chance.

It was tough to say goodbye to Singh, but it was time to move on to the white room. I was slowly coming to the middle of my journey and finally able to appreciate the great secrets being revealed to me. Even so, throughout the afternoon there were still rare occurrences that made me wonder if this were just some kind of random event or if Kris had a master plan in mind.

I made my way down to the white room, which was around the corner down an L-shaped hallway. Now that the Christmas lights were hanging, navigating my way was no problem.

The door swung open, revealing a young man with long hair who was covered in tattoos on both his arms and neck. My initial reaction was that here was someone who'd spent time in prison or was in a gang – and that I'd receive a verbal beating again – or worse – as I did with Singh.

"I'm Lucas – good to meet you, Joe."

I shook Lucas' hand, feeling a little shocked by what I saw. Lucas was probably in his late teens or early twenties, and I briefly asked myself what I could possibly learn from this kid. But after having had the gift of tolerance revealed to me, I set my prejudices aside to give him a chance.

The room was all white and had almost an antiseptic feel to it – like being in a hospital. There was a table with a few small boxes and some pens on it, and a chair. The Beans were on a table in the corner, as expected, along with a mirror.

Curiously, this room was similar to the red room – it had mobiles hanging from the ceiling, but they were all white crescent-shaped moons of different sizes. The movement of the moons overhead drifting in the soft breeze created a certain feeling of calm.

"Welcome to the white room, my friend! Almost makes you wanna play a little Cream, huh?" stated Lucas as he performed a few air guitar riffs. "Yeah – just like Clapton!"

Oh yeah, I thought, this was going to be fun – not! It didn't matter that the song "White Room" was released in the 1960s – I actually expected Lucas to pull out something funny to smoke.

"Well, Lucas – what's it going be? Are we gonna listen to some hard rock rather than Christmas music?" I quipped, sarcastically. "And if so, I wish I'd known – I left my 8-tracks at the shelter."

"Hey, you're pretty funny for a homeless guy," chuckled Lucas. "No – no rock music, but you *are* going to write out Christmas cards. First, though, I wanna show you some of my tattoos."

Implausibly, Lucas began identifying some of the ink on his body. I have to admit, it was tough to concentrate on it – I was still thinking about the Christmas cards. Was he for real?

I've never been one to get a tattoo and, frankly, it never made much sense to me. I don't know if it was the era I was born in or maybe it was just something I never understood. Maybe because it shows one's individuality and uniqueness – something I always thought I had in short supply.

Lucas proudly offered some of his better tattoos and the reasoning behind them. "Here's a great one," he said as he took off his shirt and displayed the astonishing amount of ink on his back. "This is the Phoenix – have you heard of it? I got it to commemorate immortality – not of the physical body – but of the spiritual soul and all that we leave behind on the planet when we die."

It was definitely a beautiful piece of work, made even more so by the meaning behind it.

"I believe we can truly *be* immortal, Joe. We can affect every single person we interact with if that is our desire, yet you hear about people who say they lead empty lives. Everything we create in this lifetime can live on forever."

I nodded my head in approval, partly because I didn't know what to say and partly because I couldn't believe the wisdom coming out of Lucas' mouth. It was quite a juxtaposition – having Lucas follow Singh – but it did illustrate that wisdom can come in all shapes and sizes.

"Here's my favorite, though."

He pointed to a snake that slithered its way from his shoulder all the way down to his elbow. It was an amazing piece of artistry.

"Why a snake?" I inquisitively asked.

"The snake signifies renewal because it sheds its skin," Lucas stated as he put his shirt back on. "This tattoo came at a time when I was going through my own renewal and shedding of my psychological skin."

I wanted to ask Lucas what he'd meant by that – was he in prison for a time – but I didn't want to appear crass.

"Maybe you'll want to get your own snake tattoo when you're done here, huh Joe?"

"I just might do that. I wonder if the artists make house calls to the shelter."

We both chuckled.

"Alright, Joe – we gotta get moving – it's time for the Christmas cards"

"I don't understand what you're talking about. What Christmas cards?"

"The ones on the table, of course."

Sure enough, there were Christmas cards on the table. Lucas instructed me to have a seat as he opened up the boxes that had been put there earlier.

"You should probably know that I left my address book at the shelter," I added in a comical voice.

"These are special Christmas cards – they aren't for sending out holiday greetings to your friends and family – but for you to identify the people who you believe wronged you and who you hold resentment towards."

"Let me see if I have this right – you want me to write a card to every person who I think has treated me unfairly in some way? What makes you think there is anyone?"

"Joe – seriously – you're a man filled with rage. It might surprise you that I know that, but it's difficult for you to hide it. It's written all over your face – it's in your posture. I think the question you should ask yourself is who *don't* you think treated you unfairly."

I sat there stunned – that I was listening to this young kid analyze me as if he had a doctorate in psychology. Was it really that obvious?

"My own parents disowned me when I was 16 because I wouldn't finish high school," Lucas offered. "It seemed that no matter what I did, I couldn't please them – I was never good enough. They were college folks and could never accept my belief that high school was antiquated, so I had to go live with my grandparents."

"I didn't know it at the time, but I had such feelings of abandonment and I built up so much anger that no matter what I tried to do, I'd fail and then blame them for it."

My mind was racing through the many events in my life as Lucas spoke. I saw what he was getting at. Who was I kidding? – if I sat there and actually listed everyone who I was angry with I would be there for hours. I mean, who wasn't I angry at?

I reluctantly started to compile the list. Most of what I wrote weren't really names, but entities. I wasn't angry at just one competitor – I was angry at all my competitors. Of course, I had to throw the government in there too – I mean, I was living on the street – who else was to blame?

There was the usual list of names of people I had once worked both for and with – who doesn't hate some of the back stabbers that one runs into while slaving away in the corporate world?

I listed my wife, but then thought better of it and scratched her name out. Even though I was unwilling to leave our home at first, I kind of accepted it as punishment for not giving her the life I'd once promised her.

Finally, I listed an all-encompassing collection of ethnic groups. It was telling that my blood began to boil as I did it. I never understood why I felt the way I did – it's not like I'd been wronged by any specific individual – it was almost as if I were part of some form of mass hysteria.

I dropped my pen on the table and Lucas arrived as if on cue.

"For your tranquility, Joe."

I stood up and took the white box from Lucas as I walked over to the mirror. Somewhat absentmindedly, I also took the list of names I'd just compiled. I popped the white Bean into my mouth – closed my eyes as I chewed – and waited.

"What do you feel?" Lucas asked.

I opened my eyes to the vision in the mirror. My slovenly, rage-infested appearance, set against the all white background, lent itself to a freaky sight – it was almost as if an apparition had appeared.

Then the miracle happened. The raging red aura that enveloped me – the one that Monica had alluded to – appeared to dissipate in front of my very eyes, leaving in its place a hint of something clean and neutral – white goodness. It was unfathomable; a feeling I couldn't really describe.

I crinkled up the paper that held the list of names in my hand – the names that I'd deemed guilty for my life's failures – and mentally sent them into oblivion.

"I just want to accept responsibility."

"The fourth Bean of Wisdom is the White Bean of Forgiveness. Life without forgiveness – is no life at all. Forgiveness allows us to eliminate the anger and resentment we have for others, as well as release the necessary inner energy we need to achieve our purpose."

"It's important to not just have tolerance, but to forgive yourself and others when things break down – as can happen at any moment. I'm sure you've heard the saying 'forgive them for they know not what they do.' People are people – and they come with faults."

"I'm constantly judged by my tattoos," Lucas said with a hint of irritation. "People always think I'm some kind of gangster and discriminate against me when I interact with them, like when I go for a job. It can either give me another excuse to express my failure as anger or another reason to believe in myself – it's my choice."

The cold, hard embarrassing truth was that I was also one of the people who discriminated against tattooed folks.

"But, Lucas," I pushed back, "some people don't deserve forgiveness, correct? Like those who take advantage of us or screw us over in some manner?"

"Just because you forgive someone who hurts you doesn't mean you have to do business with them again – the power is in releasing the pent-up negative energy."

"The biggest reason people have trouble forgiving others is because that requires taking responsibility – for their own shortcomings and failures in life. That snag allows them to remain passive rather than empower themselves to take action."

"Let me ask you this, Joe – did you put yourself on the list of people who've wronged you? Haven't you been your own worst enemy in life?"

Of course, I hadn't, and of course I had been.

"Forgiving yourself is powerful and necessary for any growth and success to happen. It's by far the most important type of forgiveness you can achieve. No longer will you feel the urge to beat yourself up over missed deadlines or procrastination. You can live in daily tranquility."

"Joe, you learned earlier that the rose has its faults – its prickles – but that doesn't prevent people from admiring its beauty. As a great leader you also have to realize that your employees not only have their own faults and shortcomings, but also their beauty, like the rose."

"Be a mentor for your employees. Teach them the gift of forgiveness, so when they fail to achieve on the job – not reaching their sales goals or not executing a critical project – they can accept the results and move on."

I had some ambivalence about accepting wisdom from Lucas because of his age, although I intuitively knew it shouldn't matter. However, more mixed were the feelings I had about accepting responsibility for my life. It sounded like a simple idea, but I knew it was a complex process.

Imagine not being able to blame another soul for your situation in life – realizing that you're exactly where you are today because of every decision you've ever made. It was a scary thought indeed.

"The fourth Bean of Wisdom is the Bean of Forgiveness. Forgiveness allows us to eliminate the anger and resentment we have for others, as well as release the necessary inner energy we need to achieve our purpose."

7 | Green

Being accountable for my life was a much bigger deal than I'd anticipated. The more I contemplated it, the more alarming it became. So, if I was fully responsible for *my* life, it also meant that I was entirely responsible for everyone else in my life – including my wife and sons.

These sorts of realizations are much better received when things are going well than when you're alone on the streets. It pained me to think of the damage I'd already caused my family.

It also made me understand why I'd encountered some of the failures I did in my business. In a way, I'd given myself permission to fail, because in my mind, it was all someone else's fault. Having the secret of forgiveness revealed to me reminded me of that movie campaign I'd seen some years ago that said: "this time it was personal" – it put the responsibility back on my shoulders – where it rightfully belonged.

I said goodbye to Lucas and went on my way. I was finding it more and more difficult to bid farewell to these people I was meeting because I didn't know if I'd ever see them again. How could I properly thank them for all they'd done, especially since the impact from all of it wouldn't be fully understood until I had the perspective of time.

The green room was right across the hall from the white room, which made it a breeze to get to. After a couple of knocks at the door it was opened by a middle-aged woman dressed in a green holiday outfit.

"Hello, Joe – I'm Emma."

Emma and I immediately embraced in a friendly hug that removed most of the apprehension I'd felt previously as I approached the rooms.

Emma was extremely engaging, one of those people that others instantly like. She wasn't so beautiful, physically, but wisdom radiated from her eyes and her smile felt absolutely authentic.

Emma had a disarming personality that provided a good respite from Lucas' sometimes over-the-top shtick. I felt her contentment – it enveloped her and permeated the entire room.

I entered the room and immediately collapsed under the room's mystical and intriguing spell. The only lights in the room were green-colored candles, strategically placed throughout. They made me feel like I might be in store for something truly special.

Soft, ethereal sounding music peacefully and serenely bathed the room. There was also a touch of light incense, although I didn't recognize the aroma despite my attempts to do so.

Something that suspiciously resembled a massage table took up the center of the room. If I were right, it would be a welcome relief for the debilitating aches I began having once I started living life "on the road."

"Joe, I want you to consider this your sanctuary for the short time you're here – forget who you are and where you came from – and just exist. Promise me that and wonderful things will happen."

I promised Emma that I would, but I must confess that deep down I didn't believe it. The entire scene – while very intimate and soothing – reminded me of days I'd passed at a luxury spa with my wife when I still had some coin in my pocket and love in my heart. Though appreciative of the journey and the psychological healing I was experiencing, the scars of the recent past were still too fresh. Perhaps it demonstrated my shallowness, but pampering my favorite girl always made me feel like a man in that she got to feel like a woman in ways I could never grant.

Emma instructed me to lie face down on the table, relax every muscle, and allow my pain from living to dissolve.

"A massage is a form of meditation for the body, Joe – it removes all the momentary stress of life and puts you in a state of spiritual openness. Close your eyes and allow yourself to drift away."

"I want you to wiggle your toes now, Joe, and just concentrate on every muscle's movement as if no other part of your body exists." Emma directed.

I felt kind of foolish to do it – especially since I couldn't remember the last time I'd washed my feet – but I played along with her request as best I could. I focused my attention on a nearby candle and unconsciously used its flame as a metronome for my toe movements.

"Now, slowly wiggle your fingers and feel those muscle movements, too."

I gave it my best to do exactly what Emma asked, but found it extremely difficult to comply. I knew who I was – where I was – and, unfortunately, what I was.

It was then – as I watched the colorful flame revel in its fiery dance – that I had an enlightening thought about my situation. It occurred to me over several moments – that the reason for my lack of awareness was that I couldn't turn my mind off.

No matter how hard I fought to just exist, the voices in my head wouldn't cease talking, though I won't embarrass myself by disclosing exactly what they were saying. Suffice it to say, it wasn't anything encouraging.

Emma then placed her hands on my back and put pressure on several areas, identifying points of anguish I'd never known existed. I believe I resisted at first, but gradually allowed myself to dissolve into my surroundings – becoming one with the music, fire and incense. It was intoxicating.

Something finally happened that hadn't happened for what seemed like an eternity – the voices were gone. The constant chatter that appeared to run 24/7 and tell me just how terrible I was – disappeared.

It's amazing sometimes how silence can jump out at you as easily as a loud sound – and that it can be just as deafening. The audio disturbances that continually clanged around in my head and thwarted my goals – and my dreams – telling me what a failure I was and that I could never be a success again were gone, if only briefly.

The revelation reminded me of when I would stay in my apartment surrounded by the constant roar of the big city outside. There would be moments when I'd realize I no longer heard the noise because I was so concentrated on something else – and then I'd notice the silence.

Emma continued her massage for what seemed like an hour, but was probably much less time. The voices were absent from my mind as she worked my arms and legs – and psyche. I've had many massages in my life, but nothing like this one, where I just melted into the incredible hidden universe we live in.

Emma finished and I put my torn socks and worn shoes back on, all the while in a state of bliss. I was in one of those zones where I didn't think of anything, I just existed. A zone that I'd read about many times, but was never fortunate enough to experience for myself – until now.

I jumped off the table and gazed in wonder at the surreal setting. It was hard to believe that I was in the same exact room as when I'd first gotten onto the table – it felt like my surroundings had transformed into a different environment.

Emma approached and placed a green box into my hand.

"For your spirit, Joe."

I looked into Emma's eyes for a moment before I accepted the box. We gazed intently at each other – and there were traces of tears in both of our eyes – as if we shared a telepathic moment.

I reached for the box and walked over to the usual spot in front of the mirror. I placed the Bean in my mouth – and waited.

"What do you feel?" Emma asked.

What I felt was incredible. Dozens of images flashed through my brain, similar to when in a film, a character who's dying sees their past life flash before their eyes.

I saw early morning birds fly high and I felt their plight as they searched for food to feed their babies. I felt the joy and wonder of my two little boys – laughing as two-year-olds – as they played in the sandbox, totally oblivious to the anguish in the world around them.

I opened my eyes and looked at the poor soul in the mirror, never expecting the image that stared back at me to be right there with its own sense of wonder.

"I just want to feel and experience another being."

"The fifth Bean of Wisdom is the Green Bean of Compassion. Life without compassion – is no life at all. Compassion allows us to experience – and be – in the moment with another being. Not just in pain, but also in joy."

"Compassion is not just about sorrow – it's about being in the moment with another person. Totally identifying with what they must be experiencing – joy, pain, love, creativity – a child's sense of wonder, a college student's stress over finals or the immense creativity that goes into a piece of art or writing."

"Don't get hung up on the word, Joe. Using the traditional definition just for sorrow is missing the other half of life that is joy. Focus on the emotional experience and not on the logic."

"Compassion is not intellectual understanding, such as empathy – it's a complete, unconscious, emotional oneness. There isn't a person and an event – there's no labeling of what's happening – there just is."

"The stronger our personal awareness of what another person's feeling, the deeper and more immediate our compassion is," Emma continued. "It's very tricky to compassionately feel what childbirth is like unless you've experienced it."

"Either way, you have to quiet the mind to get to true compassion for someone. It's hard to discern the powerful emotions at play when you've got a cacophony of white noise playing inside your head."

I listened to Emma and soaked in every word as she calmly filled the room with sense.

"Now that you've received the gift of compassion, Joe, you will never look at the world the same again. You'll see the fruits of far-reaching creativity and may even experience deep feelings of appreciation for the doubt, suffering, tears and time it took to create."

"As a great leader, it's imperative for you to realize that compassion can be as simple as being empathetic. You might consider others' situations and realize that one of your employees is having a bad day or is experiencing a period of great pain and doubt – or that an irate customer behaves a certain way because of a tragedy in their family or some deep fear about how they'll continue to house, clothe and feed their family.

"Compassion isn't something you just express in times of sorrow, as I've already stated. You can also express it during times of joy. It's easy for a leader to be compassionate in times of sorrow – we've all experienced our own pain. However, great leaders can separate their own egos from an event and express great compassion in times of elation."

Emma and I quietly stood eye to eye again before we embraced – it felt like a transcendent event in itself.

I was quite emotionally – and physically – shaken as I prepared to leave this great room – and experience. There was no doubt in my mind that I now knew what deep joy was – and that I might possibly be a great leader again one day – because I felt it then in every fiber of my body.

"The fifth Bean of Wisdom is the Bean of Compassion. Compassion allows us to experience – and be – in the moment with another being. Not just in pain, but also in joy."

8

Blue

I couldn't stop thinking about what had just been revealed to me. It was exciting to have a new understanding of compassion, to understand that it wasn't just a word for pain, but also, for tremendous joy; for elation. It made me realize just how out of touch I'd been with my employees. How could I truly have cared about them if I could never identify, emotionally, with what they were feeling during critical times in their lives?

I thought back about the times with my wife and how she tolerated my lack of true compassion. I must have been difficult to live with, being so totally consumed by my business and my problems – and the white noise inside my head. It'd been a rare exception, indeed, when I felt exactly what my wife was experiencing.

I was still affected by the remarkable insights and feelings I'd experienced when I ate the green Bean. The birds' flight overhead in the morning in search for food – was something I'd thought about many times as I also scrounged around for my next meal.

To see my boys as two-year-olds again – living in a state of total bliss moved me – while the world around them verges on becoming lost or self-destructing in these scary and confused times. I thought deeply about all this as I walked down the hall.

I went to the blue room and gave the door two knocks. It opened slowly and a bright, blue light streaked out of it as if a leak had sprung. Once I saw who was behind the door I knew I'd be in good hands.

"Jerry!"

"Hey, Boss!"

We gave each other a "man hug" like we were old friends.

Jerry was a much larger man up close. He looked more jovial and less businesslike than he did in the limo. I got the feeling that Jerry got his smarts from the streets rather than from a university.

The blue room evoked an otherworldly feeling in me – as if I'd been there before, maybe in one of my dreams. The walls were blue, of course, and so was the ceiling, suggesting the open air. There may even have been clouds painted on it.

This room seemed to be the kitchen of the house – at least the kind one sees in extended stay hotels – there was a stove, oven and a small refrigerator. A large table in the center of the room had what appeared to be – implausibly – cookware and baking ingredients? There were also blue boxes on a table in a corner of the room – and again, I assumed those were the Beans.

"You baking, Jerry?"

"I come from a large family who love to eat. I grew up poor, but my mama would somehow always find a way to make the greatest meals for us," Jerry reminisced. "What I loved the most was when she baked cupcakes. There's something special about cupcakes to a little boy, don't you think, Boss?"

I had to agree with Jerry, and we shared a laugh. Suddenly – for just a moment – my mind flipped back to the good times at home and I could see my two little boys excitedly grabbing cupcakes off the kitchen table. I remembered how I looked at my wife and smiled as Coffee and Cocoa licked the frosting off their cupcakes, always getting a dab or two on their noses.

"To answer your question – no, *you're* baking. I have everything here that you need – cake mix, baking pan, frosting – you a chocolate or vanilla type of guy? I have both. Me – I'm chocolate all the way – something about vanilla that just doesn't seem right."

"Chocolate, Jerry. I'm chocolate all the way – cake and frosting."

"You've made cupcakes before, right Boss? It's easy – just follow the recipe."

"You gonna help me or are you just gonna stand there and make stupid comments?"

"I'm helping – I'm helping. At least this time there's no ladder involved, right?"

Even though I'd obviously baked cupcakes before, I followed the directions on the back of the box exactly since I knew each mix had its own requirements for ingredients, baking temperature, etc.

The thought of me, a homeless man – baking cupcakes on Christmas Eve – made me chuckle because it was so ridiculous. But the more I got into it, the less ridiculous it felt. It brought me back to the times I lent a hand in one of my restaurants because of understaffing.

I always felt that working in the kitchen with the bottom line, hourly wage employees was special since it gave me a rare opportunity to get to know them – to discover what was going on in their lives. But after I opened my second restaurant, I seldom did it unless I was putting out fires.

"Tell me, Boss – you're a restaurant man – what exactly is a recipe?"

I gave Jerry a crazy look because I thought he was joking.

"Are you nuts, Jerry? What do you mean, 'what is a recipe'?"

"Yeah – what's a recipe – when it's broken down to its true core?"

"What are you – a gourmet chef now? Maybe you've been watching too many of those cooking shows."

"You're not answering the question," he scowled with irritation.

"I guess you could call it a set of instructions on how to cook or bake something." "It's funny, Boss – people will follow a box recipe for cupcakes or some chicken dish a TV chef makes, but they won't follow a recipe for success from a mentor – makes you wonder how bad they really want it."

"I don't get what you're saying."

"I used to drive a limo for a successful businessman when I was just a kid," Jerry continued. "I saw how he lived and how treated people – his family, employees and customers – and I knew then that I wanted to be like him someday. He was always helping people when they were down or when they wanted advice or help with their business."

"I'll never forget the day I asked him how to go about starting my own limo business – I couldn't have been more than 22 or 23. I thought he was going to tell me I was nuts."

Jerry's voice trailed off as if he were back on the streets once again driving the limo. I could swear that I saw him wipe away a tear or two.

"What happened?" I asked.

"He told me that success leaves traces, and to watch what he did and then copy what he did well, and eliminate his mistakes. He said success is like a recipe – the traces or footprints of others who are successful just have to be replicated. I've never forgotten that, and it's served me very well in business and in life."

Jerry was one of those people who liked to talk while he worked, unlike me – I was more of a loner in the kitchen – although I never used to be that way.

"Why the restaurant business, Boss? It's tough, no? Not like driving a limo."

"Why? I can't remember, Jerry. Maybe I used to make a mean soufflé."

I wasn't direct because I had to think about it. I often wondered why, myself. It's a difficult, volatile business with lots of stress and high employee turnover – even in good times and with great leadership.

"I mean, to get to five restaurants, you had to be doing something right," Jerry added. "What happened?"

I pondered his comment and thought back to my early days in the business – when it seemed fun and exciting – when I was filled with passion, not greed. I suddenly saw that what I'd loved about the restaurant business – the food and the people – had deteriorated into a battle to grab as much money as I could in as little time as possible.

I started cutting corners – on both the food and the employees – to squeeze every ounce of profit from it that I could. Talk about recipes – turned out that one was a recipe for disaster.

I put the cupcakes into the oven and slammed the door.

"I guess I kept hoping things would change."

Jerry looked taken aback by my slamming of the door and we stood staring at each other for a few moments.

"You lost me. What do you mean by hoping things would change?"

"What don't you get? You know – I kept hoping things would change; that I'd somehow be able to turn the business around."

"And your family?"

"Yeah, my family too. I'd hoped that once the business was turned around, the home life would too."

"Boss, hoping is wishful thinking – it's what one does when one has *no* control over events. Like when my family and I are planning a picnic – I hope it doesn't rain. Or, when I'm watching the game with the guys – I hope my team wins."

"What else was I supposed to do – give up?"

"Of course not. But, believing you *can* do something eliminates the mindset of believing you *can't*."

Jerry reached over to the small table and handed me a blue box.

"For your courage, Joe"

Even though I'd gotten a little agitated, I calmly took the box from Jerry and gingerly placed the blue Bean into my mouth. I noticed that I was becoming less and less apprehensive the more Beans I encountered, and this time was no different.

"What do you feel?" Jerry asked.

It was difficult to answer him because I was overcome with a wave of anxiety – though I had no rational reason why. I recognized it as the same daily feeling I lived with when my business began to fall apart – when I just wanted to stay in bed and ignore it all – when it became too much to bear and my confidence in myself and my ability to turn things around was just draining out of me.

I opened my eyes and looked into the mirror as I had done five previous times. This time, the image staring back at me looked so different from how I was feeling – more assured, more confident. I sort of felt like it was daring me to take action.

"I just want to believe."

"The sixth Bean of Wisdom is the Blue Bean of Faith. Life without faith – is no life at all. Faith is the building block for our futures – we realize our purpose through faith. Faith is having the courage to do something without knowing how it will happen or having any guarantees that it even will."

"Faith is not hope. Hope is dreaming or wishing something to happen without effort or taking action. Faith is all about action – hope is passive."

"Great leaders don't sit around hoping that customers come into their stores to buy. They hire and train great employees, invest in marketing and inspire their team to exceed even *their* highest expectations. Then they tackle each day as if it's their last. That's because faith is present in every day of the struggle."

"Boss, I know you're an educated man and I'm just a poor kid from the streets – but, I have to knock that idea of hope out of your head. Hope has *no* business in *your* business. The moment I took hope out of my business and put my faith into it by following the recipe for success that my mentor taught me is the day my business took off."

There wasn't much I could say to Jerry at this point because, intuitively, I knew he was right. Hope had led me down a paralyzing path where, instead of taking courageous action, I passively waited – until my business – and my marriage – fell apart. I often felt there was a reason for the paralysis.

"Jerry, it's easy to say 'take action,' but what about when you don't know *what* do? Sometimes it's just easier to lie in bed and do nothing."

"I'm sure you've heard the saying 'whatever your mind can conceive, you can achieve.' Well, you don't attain the desired result by daydreaming or hoping," Jerry preached. "You don't watch the Olympics on television and state that you hope to be a future Olympian and honestly expect that result. Becoming an Olympian is a daily test of faith and living with anticipation – where despite everything, despite all the negative messages, you move ahead, a little more each day."

"What a future Olympian *does* have is a plan – a recipe, if you will – to get to where they need to go. The biggest impediment to having faith is fear – and the biggest creator of fear is ambiguity. Create a plan – any plan – and follow it faithfully."

"Having a plan creates anticipation, Boss" Jerry continued. "It creates a pattern of attraction – almost as if the universe knows what you need and magnetizes those things into your life to help you achieve your goals and dreams."

"Boss, as a great leader, you must become a mentor to your employees and give them *your* recipe for success. Instill in them the faith to move forward with their *own* transformation – their *own* dreams and goals."

"Think of it like this – you used to feed people at your restaurant with food – now you'll be feeding them with the food of life."

I took the cupcakes out of the oven and absentmindedly put vanilla frosting on the first batch, to Jerry's consternation. I applied some colorful Christmas sprinkles to top them off, and while doing that, I wondered what we were going to do with them now that they looked so inviting.

It dawned on me that – as the caterpillar possesses the faith to transform itself into a butterfly – I also had to base my transformation, my fulfilling of my purpose – on faith.

"The sixth Bean of Wisdom is the Bean of Faith. Faith is the building block for our futures – we realize our purpose through faith. Faith is having the courage to do something without knowing how it will happen or having any guarantees that it even will."

9

Black

It was quite a liberating moment when I discovered that much of what I'd done most of my life – hope for success – was entirely different from having faith. I felt empowered by feeling that my future results were within my control rather than always expecting miracles to happen.

It made me think back to my family and of how I'd hoped we could get through the hard times – rather than having the faith to move forward without having all the answers all the time.

I imagined what faith would've done for my restaurant business if I'd had the courage to move forward despite being without a clue about how I'd accomplish anything.

I closed the door behind me and made my way to the black room as instructed, where again, I discovered the door ajar. I knocked twice and entered after receiving no answer. Black certainly wasn't a misnomer because the room was nearly dark except for a sliver of sunlight cracking through the shades.

I stood near the doorway, afraid to move forward in case I bumped into something. The darkness felt more disorienting than what I'd experienced when I first entered the building, as if someone or something were watching and about to jump out at me – or had I watched too many horror movies in the past?

"Hello?" I called out.

After no answer for what felt like minutes, but was probably several seconds, I turned to leave the room.

"Back here!" a voice shouted.

Immediately, a shade rose slightly on the rear window, almost illuminating the figure of a man dressed in black sitting in the back of the room. It gave me a creepy feeling and goose bumps splayed across my body. I couldn't make out much about him, but what little sunlight there was, danced off of what appeared to be a medallion on his chest.

"Giving up already?" his deep voice questioned.

I didn't know how to answer, so I didn't. Instead, I quickly scanned the room's interior looking for clues as to what I was in for.

The walls were painted black, which gave the room the feeling of a cave. And though I expected to see the walls covered with macabre artifacts, they were lined with pictures, trophies and ribbons.

Several items were scattered around the room, similar to what you'd see in a retail store – a child's bicycle, a skateboard, a guitar, golf clubs, toy cars – and baby shoes! There were also some large, weird looking items leaning against the back wall – were those skis?

It wasn't until the man began to roll towards me that I saw he was a paraplegic in a wheelchair. The man – probably in his late 20s – was clean cut and had an athletic frame.

"The name's JJ."

"Joe," I replied, as I went to shake his hand and was left hanging.

"I know who you are. You're the guy I just saw about to walk out the door. You call yourself a leader?" JJ gushed. "You must have quite a following."

It was clear that here was a classic, bitter military veteran who was going to hammer me with the same ferocity he probably took out on his enemies.

"I'm sorry JJ, maybe now's not a good time."

"A good time for what? For losing?" JJ mocked. "Poor baby – do you want to leave and go back to the homeless shelter where it's nice and safe?"

"There's a reason why I'm the last stranger you're going to meet. I'm not like all the others who basically threw softballs up for you to hit. No, you have to prove to me you've got what it takes to continue."

Oh yeah, JJ was good. Despite the verbal tongue-lashing I got, I couldn't help seeing the medal on his chest. Surprisingly, it was not the military medal I'd expected, but something else.

"Yeah, that's an Olympic skiing medal. Surprised?"

It became painfully obvious that I couldn't win this. JJ was a jaded man who, through some unfortunate experience, lost his legs, but continued to live in the past.

"I questioned Kris when I heard that he'd chosen you – a quitter who'd left his wife and kids," he continued. "Tell me – how *does* one leave two little boys?"

I didn't have the heart – or courage – to tell JJ that it was a mutual decision between my wife and I for me to leave. Not that it would matter, of course. His mind was already made up. However, the tension between us was making me sick and I just wanted to – dare I think it? – leave.

Suddenly, though, the old Joe came back – the one who wouldn't back down from a confrontation in the good ole days.

"Look man, I don't want any trouble. Obviously, you've already made up your mind that I'm a loser. But I'm not the one living in the past – *you* are. You lost your legs and dream of being a skier, so you get your kicks making life miserable for everyone else."

I got right into his face.

"That about right, JJ?"

JJ backed his wheelchair away and then did something very strange – he smiled, and then offered up a chuckle.

"I have to laugh. You think this medal and those trophies are from *before* I lost my legs?"

"They're not?" I added incredulously.

JJ removed the medal from his chest and put it in my hand..

"Take a look for yourself."

I can't remember ever holding anything in my hand that was so magnificent – and meant so much. Every person in the world understands the work and dedication that goes into becoming an Olympian. I couldn't fathom what it would take to become a Gold Medal Paralympian.

"It's beautiful," I blurted.

"Anyone can be a skiing champion when they have legs," JJ added casually. "How is that special?"

I suddenly understood that here was a man of considerable substance and fortitude.

"How did you lose your legs?" I cautiously asked.

"It's amazing what crazy things a teenager will do with a car. But, I had a dream to become an Olympic skiing champion and legs – or no legs – wasn't gonna stop me."

"I'm sorry I went off on you – a man of your courage."

"Courage? I don't have any more courage than the person who wonders everyday how he's going to feed his family and pay his bills. That person persists because he has no other choice except to give up."

I listened quietly to JJ's words, probably more so because they resonated with my current situation.

A few moments of silence ensued and then I heard it. Maybe it'd been present the entire time and I was too emotionally involved to notice. An unmistakable melody, whispered, like the music of angels – it was the sound of children laughing.

"Go ahead – take a look."

I rushed to the window to raise the shade – and stared out in astonishment – there was a long line of children with their parents outside the building, waiting as if for an event to begin.

"It looks like the entire town is here."

JJ rolled over to the window to see for himself.

"Hardly," he offered. "Only six year olds participate."

His remark hit me like a sledgehammer.

"Only six year olds?"

The words were barely out of my mouth when I thought about my boys.

"Yeah, that was the way it was performed centuries ago – to maintain secrecy and exclusivity, and the same tradition continues today," JJ remarked.

I wondered if it was possible to call my boys and notify them of this great, once-in-a-lifetime opportunity, but wrote off the idea because it was just too late. Or – more likely – maybe I was afraid that if I contacted my wife after all these months she'd tell me to get lost.

"There's a reason why this building is where it is. It's not supposed to be easy to find, otherwise it wouldn't be special. Children and their parents not only *want* to be here – they *have* to be here – like those people in that science fiction movie."

I assumed JJ meant the movie, "Close Encounters of the Third Kind," where hundreds of people went on a spiritual quest to find an alien spacecraft. It was also one of my favorite movies – I'd often wished I were the one that got to go on that spacecraft.

JJ moved the modified skis that were leaning against the wall, and I saw a mirror and a small table with the Bean boxes.

"For your journey, Joe."

I gladly took the black box from JJ since now I'd done this several times before. However, I somehow sensed that this time it was more than that – almost like a graduation or a capstone, if you will, for the entire education I'd just received.

I chewed the black Bean for several seconds in anticipation of its effect. I chewed and chewed – but I felt no reaction.

"What do you feel?" JJ asked.

I probably relished the black Bean longer than any of the previous six Beans because I wasn't quite convinced of my lack of response. Unlike the other times, I felt no great internal event – no powerful emotions; nothing.

I opened my eyes and looked at myself in the mirror for what would be the last time that day. I stood there in silence – waiting for a reaction or for *something* to happen like each time before. It didn't come.

Then I realized that *that* was exactly what was supposed to happen. I looked at my image in the mirror and no longer saw that scared, unrecognizable man in the purple room or that unloved man in the red room. This person peering back at me wasn't lacking something – he *had* something.

"I just want to do great things. For myself ... for my family ... and for the world."

"The seventh – and last– Bean of Wisdom is the Black Bean of Perseverance. Life without perseverance – is no life at all. It's the key to everything we do. Our sense of purpose, our skills and our talents are like the ingredients of a great meal. We must give ourselves the time to cook, just as we would a soufflé, because each one of us is on our own timeline."

"Nothing matters without perseverance. If purpose is the engine that drives the boat, perseverance is the rudder that steers it and keeps it in the water."

"It's mind-blowing that people will work for 10 or 20 years to climb the corporate ladder of a company, but will only give themselves three months before giving up on their own business – their own dreams. Artists can even be worse – give them a rejection or two from either a stranger or a loved one and they might put their dreams on the shelf for years."

"Great leaders persevere in tough times. Look at what I've accomplished with no legs, Joe. Imagine what *you* can do with two."

JJ rolled over to where the baby shoes were and flung them my way, daring me to catch them before they hit me in the face.

"Have you ever met a child who doesn't walk because they gave up trying? It doesn't happen, does it? They'll fall a hundred times, but each time, they'll get back up on those wobbly legs and give it another shot."

JJ rolled the bike towards me.

"Ever ride a bike, Joe? Stupid question, right? How many times do you think a kid falls off their bicycle when they're learning to ride, but gets right back on despite their scrapes and bruises because they know they can conquer it. Where are your scrapes and bruises, Joe? When are you going to get back on your life path and fulfill your purpose?"

"Look at all this stuff around the room – skateboard, golf clubs, guitar, cars – all of these things take perseverance to learn to control. No one's born knowing this stuff. Yet, how often do people think about giving up on their dreams or everything they believe in? The Beans of Wisdom have continued only because of perseverance."

"The same can be said about leadership. You hear about people being born leaders, but that's nothing but crap. A person works at it the same way someone works at playing the guitar or learning the game of golf. It takes perseverance, self-discipline and the passion to go on."

JJ's rant was over. I stood there – a bit dumbfounded – like you might be after being reprimanded for making a mistake or doing something stupid. I looked into his piercing eyes and saw the ferocity of a determined young man – who was either about to unload on me or grant me acceptance – I couldn't be sure.

"Joe, the time has now come for me to ask *you*. Are you ready? Are you willing? It takes a great man to do great things – and now you've been given the tools. You've learned that purpose, love, tolerance, forgiveness, compassion and faith are key ingredients for personal success – and that perseverance is the key to fulfillment. What you say and do will live on long after you've passed."

"How many employees can you nurture into exceptional leaders by inspiring them to not give up? To never give in to defeat because we only lose when we don't persevere? How many loved ones can you motivate to fulfill their purpose – their destiny?"

I didn't answer JJ right away. Not because I didn't know the answer – I did – but, because I was thinking back to that moment when I was in the limo with Kris. When he said that I'd have to give back for the rest of my life and I foolishly thought that I could just agree to that and in the end, walk away.

I made the commitment to myself right then – that there was no way this man was ever gonna walk away from anything again for the rest of his life.

"The seventh Bean of Wisdom is the Bean of Perseverance. It's the key to everything we do. Our sense of purpose, our skills and our talents are like the ingredients of a great meal. We must give ourselves the time to cook, just as we would a soufflé, because each one of us is on our own timeline."

10

Redemption

I stood motionless, not knowing what to say or feel. This day that started like any other – waking up in the shelter and thanking the higher powers that be that I'd lived another day to see the rising sun – had taken on a life of its own.

I couldn't help but feel how my own perseverance to survive had brought me to this moment. How my own perseverance – however meager it was to just get through the day alive – had taken me on an incredible journey that no man could imagine or could expect.

I thought back to the times I'd given up in my life – how I abandoned my dreams because I thought I wasn't good enough – or, worse – because others thought I wasn't good enough.

JJ instructed me to return to the purple room where I'd begun my journey and wait for further instructions from Kris.

I walked slowly back to where it had all started for me that afternoon. Unlike that journey that began in darkness and ambiguity, this one took place under a beautiful sky full of Christmas lights and clarity. I felt an excitement that I hadn't felt in many years. It reminded me of the way you feel when something remarkable and surreal is truly happening and you just go along for the ride – without trying to label the experience or ask why.

I paced the purple room nervously, alone in deep thought. I gave the wall a swipe and saw that the paint was already dry to the touch. I brushed my fingers over the items I'd interacted with – the ladder and the paintbrush – and appreciated how my perspective had changed. What were once inanimate objects to me had become living, breathing necessities that had purpose.

Kris entered, followed by everyone else who participated in my day of receiving the Beans. The attentiveness in the room was powerful – and liberating – although no one spoke a word while they formed a line against the wall behind Kris.

I looked around and couldn't help feeling connected with all of the others. Even though no one in the room showed any kind of emotion on their faces, I had to believe that they all experienced the same sparkle.

"We've come to the last step on your journey, Joe; in many ways, the most important one," pronounced a solemn Kris. "You've experienced many things today and I told you earlier that certain occurrences would be explained as we went along. So – now, do you have any questions about what happened?"

Kris must've been kidding – all I *had* were questions. The whole thing was so overwhelming that I didn't know where to begin – so I began at the beginning.

"How do the Beans work?" I inquired. "I mean – those things I felt – how do you know how each person will respond?"

"Each person's experience is unique. Adult or child – what you feel is what is specifically important to you at that moment."

"Who put this all together? I mean, the whole operation runs more efficiently than most businesses I've seen."

Kris didn't answer right away, as if he were searching for the exact words to answer that question.

"Remember that wise man I told you about?" Kris asked. "The one who was so fed up with the way the world had become – so cynical and filled with hatred – that he began the ritual again?"

"Yes?" I answered, like a question.

"That person was me, Joe. I was the one who created all of what you see here, along with the help of many great people, including everyone here in this room. We didn't spare any expense to make sure that what we do here is as close as possible to what that secret organization did many years ago. No advertising, no social media, no going into schools – everything is done by invitation and word of mouth – just as it was done in centuries past."

I had a lump in my throat for what seemed like an eternity as I considered what he'd just told me. I peered into his deep, dark eyes, overcome by feeling – as if I were looking into the heart of this great man.

"I don't know what else to say," I stammered.

"We don't have much time, Joe. This efficient operation, as you call it, must move on, because now it's time for the most important part – the children. Remember what I told you earlier in the day while we were in the limo – about you giving back? Now it's time for you to make your decision."

Kris stared straight into my confused eyes.

"What is it you would like to do, Joe?"

I stood motionless as I processed Kris' words. Yes, I remembered what he told me and, most shamefully, what I'd thought at the time – about *not* following through on my commitment. Now it seemed like that thought had occurred ages ago – when I truly *was* a different person, and in my mind, I had now *already* committed. But … to what?

What did I want to do? All of the beautiful experiences I had just been through and would treasure forever, all of the wisdom I'd gained in such a short time – what would be the best way for me to give back?

I really wanted to tell Kris that I preferred to do what Monica, Jerry and all the others did – hand out the Beans, but I knew that I wasn't qualified. It seemed as if Kris had so perfectly chosen each of them that I couldn't imagine anyone else doing it. But I *had* to ask anyway.

"I want to do what everyone here in the room is doing – give out the Beans."

Kris remained unaffected and emotionally blank.

"You think you're ready for a position like that? To take someone from a place of unawareness to a place of understanding? I'm sorry, but that's impossible," Kris stated. "Those positions are all filled and will remain so until someone decides to retire or do something else. What else can you do?" Kris scowled.

I hesitated for a moment, since it was the first time I'd felt threatened by Kris. I knew time was short and it seemed as if he were getting impatient with me. Why I thought this would be a good time for humor is beyond me, but I assume that the pressure of the situation was what did it.

"I think I do a pretty good job of painting and hanging Christmas lights," I joked. "How about something like that?"

My answer didn't go over well and Kris remained stoic.

"Is that what you're best suited for – a man with your business background?"

I didn't know where Kris was going with this. He *knew* my business background – and it stunk.

"I guess I don't have any idea about what else is available," I added in a serious voice. "Obviously, it takes many people to put this all together. Perhaps there's something else you can recommend that I'd be able to contribute to."

My words hung in the air, and there was a palpable silence in the room for the longest time before Kris responded.

"I *do* have one opening that I believe you'd be perfect for – to give the Bean of Purpose."

I must have looked pretty stupid standing there with a blank look on my face because I couldn't believe what I'd just heard.

"I'm sorry, Kris – it sounded like you said I would be perfect for handing out the Bean of Purpose."

"I did, Joe."

I looked around at the other faces in the room to see if any of them were in on the joke and laughing, but no one moved a muscle.

"Well, I'm at a loss here, Kris. I thought *you* give out the Bean of Purpose?"

"I do," Kris deliberately spoke. "I did."

Kris moved across the room as he spoke, partially to diffuse the tension and partially so no one could see the tears forming in his eyes.

"The time has come for me to retire, Joe – and I've chosen you to be my successor and carry on the Beans of Wisdom legacy. This is my wish for you if you choose to accept it."

I don't think I heard everything Kris had just said because I felt like I was in a trance, like when you receive news just too incredible to comprehend. My eyes began to water as it hit me and I realized *what* he'd just said.

I couldn't believe it – I didn't believe it! There'd only been a few times in my life when I'd gotten such extraordinary news and those times had been long gone – when I was in a much better place. This must've been a mistake.

"You don't even know anything about me – except that I'm homeless and a failure at everything I do – whether it's in business, or as a husband and a father," I pushed back. "Why would you want me?"

"On the contrary, Joe – I know exactly everything I need to know about you and your ability to be a great leader. I know that you now have great purpose in your life and that you'll do anything to help your employees find theirs. I also know that you now love yourself unconditionally and that you'll use that love to facilitate your employees' metamorphosis."

"You've received the gift of tolerance and, now that you have it, you'll always understand and accept not just others' differences, failures and shortcomings, but also your own. You've also experienced the powerful gift of forgiveness, not just for yourself, but also for your enemies, your competitors and anyone else you held resentment for."

"The power of compassion and the experience of connecting with other human beings, not just when they're in pain or suffering, but also during their moments of great joy, is now yours. You also received the gift of faith to help you make both you and your employees' dreams come true."

"But, maybe more importantly, now that you understand the secret of perseverance, you need never allow yourself – or your employees – give up on goals and dreams. Failure only happens because you stop trying."

"Tell me, Joe – what else do I need to know about you?"

I collapsed to my knees and began to weep uncontrollably, in gratitude. I felt so weird and so joyful – it was the first time in memory that my elation didn't involve a spreadsheet, an accountant or a profit & loss statement. It was my own pure joy.

I was paralyzed on the floor, not knowing what to think or feel when a sound brought me back to the moment. What else could have happened? How else could it be explained? From beyond the walls of the room I heard unmistakable music – beautiful Christmas music.

"Do you have any questions, Joe?" Kris asked.

I got up off the ground – a bit embarrassed – and took a deep breath to regain my composure.

"I do, Kris. How will I know what to do? I don't know where to begin!"

"The most important thing at this moment is the children and the giving of the Beans. After that, you'll return the day after Christmas and begin preparations for next year. Everything that took place today has to be reversed and the rooms have to be put back to their original condition for next time – for the next person to experience, exactly as you did."

"Joe, there's no time to explain everything fully right now, but suffice it to say that you'll become the director of the foundation and be in charge of everything it stands for. Along with that responsibility comes a full support team that will train and guide you every step of the way."

Kris looked at me very seriously, as he'd done hours ago in the limo.

"I need an answer, Joe."

"Yes, I would be honored to accept, Kris."

It was one of the few times that I actually saw Kris smile. It was as if the transfer of responsibility and leadership meant as much to him as it did to me. We hugged warmly while the others clapped and cheered.

"Okay everyone, it's time," Kris ordered. "Let's get ready."

The others filed out of the room, shaking my hand in congratulations as they did.

"So what do I do tonight?" I asked.

"You? You'll give out the Bean of Purpose, of course."

Kris pulled a key out of his pocket and placed it in my hand.

"And this is so you can lock up tonight on the way out."

11

Reunion

I couldn't believe what I'd just heard him say. I was hyperventilating – because of the thrill *and* the responsibility. In some ways this commitment was greater than any I'd ever made in the world of business.

Imagine – me, a failed business owner and a severely flawed person – given another chance to make a difference. It was definitely a special day.

It provoked me to think about all the decisions I'd made to get here. Was I really in control of my destiny as I'd thought – or was there some higher power at work that led me to that soup kitchen today?

How did Kris even know I would be there for lunch? What if I'd just stayed at the homeless center all day sulking about how unfortunate I was instead of listening to my inner voice – the one inside my heart, not my head. Would my life have changed? The gratitude I felt at that moment was incalculable; I recognized just how fortunate I was to be the one chosen to lead this important mission.

I pulled the building key out of my pocket to check that I wasn't dreaming and that this was actually happening. I examined it and ran my finger over the contours of its cuts and, as I did, I realized for the first time in my life that sometimes you have to go through a lot – severe grief and miserable times – to get to the sweet part – of life.

The excitement for the start of the event began to build. It reminded me of when I fooled around with acting in college. It *did* feel like the opening night of the one and only play I was in – with the exception of everyone saying 'break a leg,' of course!

Just like in the theatre, there was a special wardrobe for the job. Kris said there was no way I could participate dressed as a homeless man, so he gave me something more fitting for the event. I always heard the saying, 'clothes make the man,' but I never really understood it until now. It's incredible how hanging different threads on a man's body can cause his self-worth to rise – as it did mine.

I felt apprehension in the air about the performances – or was it just my own performance anxiety affecting me? Although I was a little unnerved that Kris wanted me to be the one to open the door and give the first Bean, I was still aglow with the thought of it.

The time had finally come for the event to start! My mind raced back to when I was in bed that morning and how I'd reluctantly left the homeless shelter at lunchtime, without a clue about what was in store for me. Words couldn't explain how I was feeling – like I was six years old again.

With my hand on the doorknob, I paused briefly to look back at Kris. He was smiling when he gave me his nod of approval to move ahead.

I opened the door to the cries of children who jumped with joy and excitement in anticipation of what was about to happen. My eyes didn't scan the throng of children and their parents that lined the block, or the street decorations that created the festive atmosphere. No, my eyes zeroed in on the very first child in line with his mother.

"Daddy!"

There were my sons – right there in front of me after all these months.

"Mommy, it's daddy!" exclaimed Coffee.

I went down to my knees in disbelief. I've never won a lottery or anything like that, but I couldn't imagine feeling any better or any happier than I felt at that moment.

I took both of my boys into my arms and hugged them like I never had in the six years of their short lives. Tears streamed down my face as I looked up and saw my wife gazing back at me with tears also running down her cheeks.

"Daddy, the bean! Give us the magic bean," yelled Cocoa.

I broke away from the boys to hand them the purple boxes. Each chewed the Bean like it was a piece of their favorite candy.

"What do you feel?" I whispered.

"It tastes like ..."

"*Not* taste. Feel. What do you feel?"

"It feels like when I ask you and mommy why I'm here," said Cocoa.

"And where I come from," Coffee said excitedly.

"This is the Bean of Purpose," I softly spoke. "It's a gift to help you remember why you're here on Earth."

I hugged both of my boys again, intending not to ever let them go, but I knew there was more work to be done.

"Okay boys, on to the next room."

"Daddy, are you coming home today?" cried Cocoa. "I miss you."

"Mommy misses you, too," screamed Coffee. "She always says so."

"Well, I don't know boys," I said as I stood up. "It's up to mommy."

I looked into my wife's teary eyes and saw her mouth the two most wonderful words I thought I'd never see or hear again – come home.

Again I hugged both of my sons to me.

"Yes, daddy *will* be home tonight. But, you have to keep moving right now – we're holding up the whole line."

"Yay!" shouted Cocoa.

"We're a family again!" exclaimed Coffee.

I so wanted to follow the boys as they ran off to the next room to share in their discovery, but I had hundreds of other kids to serve. I hugged my wife for what felt like hours, but was no more than a second or two, before letting her escort the twins down the hall.

"Thank you," I cried.

I went on to serve what seemed like hundreds of boxes of the purple Bean, each time hearing how it felt to each little boy and girl. It was so fulfilling that I wished I could've heard how the children responded to the other colored Beans.

Engaging with the parents was almost as inspirational. Each of the parents thanked me for helping make a difference in their child's life. It was one of the most satisfying times in my whole life and I really did feel that I'd finally discovered my own purpose!

Before I knew it, the line of children dwindled down and I was serving the last child. I watched with sadness as the frenzied hallway quieted down. The children were on their way to spend Christmas Eve with their own families. And at that moment I experienced tremendous gratitude – I also had a home and a family to go to.

We celebrated the end of that amazing evening in the blue room – after all of the children had left – a short wrap party, if you will. A few of the people raved about my cupcakes, even though they knew I'd just followed a recipe – maybe that's what it was all about. It was undoubtedly the most rewarding experience of my business career to have been part of such a fantastic team.

I felt sad to see everyone put on their coats to go home and spend Christmas Eve with their families. Some of them I wouldn't see again until the next year's event. I watched as they joyously hugged one another for a job well done and bid each other a wonderful holiday.

"Merry Christmas, Boss!" said Jerry, as he bear-hugged me. "I'll be outside waiting for you."

"Merry Christmas, Jerry. Great job tonight!"

Monica was crying as she hugged me goodbye.

"Feliz Navidad! Come visit me sometime!"

"Feliz Navidad!" I said with tears in my own eyes. "Of course, I really will."

JJ rolled by, already showing his Christmas spirit with a holiday stocking atop his head.

"My ride's here, Joe – gotta go," he said, and we embraced like lifelong friends.

Emma and Lucas also stopped by to give me a hug and wish me Merry Christmas before leaving to go to their own homes.

Singh gave me an abbreviated hug.

"See – the turban doesn't bite," he said with a laugh.

"Singh, my friend. Merry Christmas! What would I have done without you?"

"Merry Christmas, Joe. As great as today was, the best is yet to come."

The group filed out the door, one by one, leaving me alone in the empty building with Kris.

"It's time to say goodbye, Joe."

I stood frozen – almost in disbelief – even though I'd known the time would come. I moved forward into Kris' outstretched his arms.

"How can I ever thank you, Kris?"

"You already did – by committing to spread the word and grow our family."

"When will I see you again?"

"I'll be around – but you don't need me – you're ready. Trust your inner voice – your vision – and let the higher powers guide you like they guided me."

I didn't want to let go of Kris – was I afraid of being on my own? Did I trust myself with his vision after having failed so many times in my own life?

"Go home, Joe. You have a wonderful family waiting for you."

"Merry Christmas, Kris."

"Merry Christmas, my friend."

My head felt as if it would explode when Kris waved goodbye and headed out the door. For the next several minutes, I walked through the rooms and relived the scenes as if after a big party. I imagined the shouts and laughter as the children moved through the rooms – now dead silent – to receive their precious gifts. I also reminisced about the joy I'd felt when I handed each of them a purple Bean.

I shut off the lights; with my hand on the doorknob, I glanced down the hallway. It was quiet and dark, exactly how it'd been when I first entered the building. It felt so different there, now after all that had happened.

I stepped into the crisp December air and noticed that it was snowing – exactly as Singh had predicted! There were a few stragglers sprinting through the snow and throwing snowballs at each other. What a wonderful evening it'd been for the kids! It made me remember what George said earlier, during lunch – something special *does* always happen on Christmas Eve – we just have to look for it.

I covered myself against the cold wind and carefully made my way down the now icy stairs into the waiting limo. Once inside, I rolled down the window so I could soak in the beautiful scene that seemed created just for me.

"Stop the car!" I shouted to Jerry.

I poked my head out the window to get a better look at something that, just hours ago meant nothing to me. Now attached to the pole, barely visible with snow sticking to it was the street sign: Wisdom Lane.

I felt sad to think how it would be another 365 days before I would experience this event again, though never again the same way. At the same time, it made me smile to think I'd be back after Christmas to begin preparations for the next year's batch of six year olds.

For one moment – a flash – I wondered if I should get a snake tattoo to represent my own transformation and renewal as Lucas suggested. I figured a small, inconspicuous one couldn't hurt – it would be my little secret with the world. But then I decided to put off the decision until the new year.

"Take me home, Jerry."

"You got it, Boss!"

I thought a lot during the ride home. I relived many of the day's extraordinary experiences with my new friends and, of course, with my family. I felt that not only had I become a better leader, but I'd become a better husband, a better father – a better man.

I mulled over the enormity of the task that was ahead of me and saw it was really too big for one person to handle. I began to dream big – perhaps even more so than Kris had ever done. I asked myself, 'why limit the Beans to just those children in the city? What if we could spread the message to all the children … in the world?'

It's an audacious idea – and it could work – but only with your help. If I could get your commitment to spread the word about the Beans of Wisdom, imagine what we could accomplish together during the next 365 days. Can I count on you? I know the children of the world will ...

THE END

12

Epilogue

Joe on beans of wisdom

It has now been several years since my incredible journey of discovery facilitated by the Beans of Wisdom. My boys grew up to become teenagers and young men that I have faith in to do great things in the world. It hasn't always been easy but, as JJ said, they're on their own paths now and they'll each find and serve their unique purpose on their own particular timelines.

The wonderful thing about great memories is that they endure forever – I'll always remember my boys as those two year olds who played in their sandbox, filled with wonder. I only hope that I can live up to their idea of what a great father is.

My wife and I reconciled and are now living the life of our dreams – experiencing and being present for each other in every precious moment. That's all you need when you've married your soul mate – everything else in life is a bonus.

I've participated in a number of Beans of Wisdom Christmas Eve moments since becoming its director, and I'm continually humbled by their magic and power and the extraordinary people, both adults and children, that I meet.

Although it was a watershed moment in my life, the Beans were not so easy to implement at first. I'm not going to say that I came out of the event as a perfect leader – or man. We humans are flawed. Thus, change doesn't occur immediately – and great change sometimes takes a long time.

The important thing to know is that you must take that first step and get onto your own path – as Dorothy did on the Yellow Brick Road in the "Wizard of Oz" – and believe that great things can happen once your transformation begins to take shape.

The butterfly doesn't understand how its transformation will manifest; nature mandates that it enter its chrysalis stage – its protected growth and differentiation stage – so that its metamorphosis can take place. You, like the butterfly, must also enter your own chrysalis and trust that your true purpose will become manifest.

Leadership principles have come quite a long way since my extraordinary experience. It seems like every day I read about another leadership story on a blog or social media website. A brief internet search today identified several stories published over the last week, including some from notable authors.

Articles such as the "10 Traits of a Great Boss," and "12 Attributes Every Great Leader Has," make for great reading, especially when one notices that they have most of the qualities expressed in the piece. I read these articles myself, closely examining the characteristics to see whether or not I was determined to be a great leader – at least on that day until a new article comes out the next day.

The fact is that all of these articles are true to an extent. However, just because you have the traits doesn't guarantee that you will be a great leader, or that if you don't have them, that you would be a bad leader. These articles tend to compare the attributes they mention with the character of various great thought leaders of our time – and the paradox is that there may also be some terrible leaders who share these traits. In fact, thought leaders themselves are typically complex, extraordinary individuals who have manifested their life's purpose on such a grand scale that it does them – and anyone else – a disservice to make such comparisons.

What's important to realize is that human beings are complex, and someone we call a great leader today may have a composite of basic, critical, attributes – along with a few specialized attributes mixed in.

It would be the same principle if one were to investigate major-league baseball pitchers. There are many great pitchers in the League, past and present. Each pitcher must have the basic necessary skills – typically a wicked fastball – to make it to the League.

However, each pitcher usually has a few other incredible pitches, including their "go to" specialty pitch, in their repertoire. The same principle applies to leadership.

For me, the Beans of Wisdom opened my eyes to what essential human qualities a great leader must have to be successful in life. These essentials are crucial, just as good soil and nutrients are critical for a rose to develop strong roots and as a result, yield beautiful blooms.

Leaders lacking these basic human attributes can add whatever leadership qualities are currently in vogue, but there will always be an element missing from their end product. That element, in most cases, is authenticity.

I am sometimes told as I speak on the topic that the Beans appear "touchy-feely" and don't really address leadership principles. In support of the Beans I always mention the associate engagement surveys that many companies administer to take the pulse of their workforce's level of job satisfaction and, just as importantly, the effect of leadership on the work environment. I present the following composite survey questions for your understanding:

Does the work I do have meaning? (purpose)

Do I feel that my contributions make a difference? (love) Can I succeed without sacrificing aspects of my personality or culture? (tolerance)

Does this company care about its employees? (compassion)

Am I consistently challenged by my responsibilities? (forgiveness)

Do I continually have opportunities to learn new skills? (faith)

Do I know what is required of me to advance within the company? (perseverance)

It is clear that, while these articles make for great reading, what is measured by companies has very little to do with the traits one typically reads about.

I am also often asked how one goes about acquiring the attributes of the Beans if one doesn't currently convey them. That's a good question – and better answered by someone more qualified than me. For that reason, I've asked seven friends to say a few words about how they implemented the secrets and power of the Beans in the hope that it contributes to your understanding and the development of your own metamorphosis.

Let me leave you with this: the magic of the Beans – and a unique, authentic and fulfilling life – is available to everyone. No person or entity has a monopoly on life – nonetheless, you *do* have jurisdiction over your own life.

There's a great proverb that says 'the best way to predict one's future is to create it.' You're an extraordinary individual – despite what you may currently think or feel. Become the main character in your own life story – don't relegate yourself to taking a bit part or walk-on role.

Your answer is there – that voice inside you – as it has probably been for years.

Kris on purpose

I've been retired for several years now since my last Beans of Wisdom gathering when I turned the key over to my successor – and one of life's great leaders, Joe.

Retirement is not all one reads about – both good and bad. There's more time, of course, to do the things I always wanted to do. Unfortunately, many people often don't know what they want to do – or what they desire doesn't turn out to be or manifest their real purpose.

I've been able to spend more time with my family and those I love. I've seen my children grow to become great leaders in the world – while oftentimes stumbling along as humans often do. While the magic of the Beans is often talked about in regard to leadership, they also come in handy for moms or dads – or anyone else.

I still spend time lecturing around the world. It pains me to see that there are so many unhappy people everywhere today – yet it also gives me great joy that there are just as many who want to better the world but just don't yet know how.

This is the greatest time in life for someone to do what they were put on this earth to do – to fulfill their purpose. Spreading your message – your voice – so that others can hear it around the globe has never been so achievable at any other time.

The power of the Beans lies in the fact that they are designed to work in harmony with one another. There is a logical order. It's no accident that the Bean of Purpose is the first Bean because once you discover your true purpose, the world opens up to you – and life flows.

If you aren't living your true purpose – if your occupation isn't your true calling – or doesn't in some way complement your true calling, you'll never be at your best. How can you be a great leader when you have trouble leading yourself? You'll always feel as if something's missing and your sense of your own authenticity will always be a struggle.

It's difficult to exhibit transcendent love towards others when you're miserable in your job and in your life. Consequently, if you can't exhibit authentic love, how can you ever offer true compassion and forgiveness to others?

The question I get asked most often is how a person can discover their true purpose – their destiny. There are so many mixed messages in today's media that it's very difficult to hear your inner voice among all the white noise. Sometimes it seems that this world is insane and that thousands of people – and entities – are competing for your attention.

It's hard to know what to do or who to turn to. Many people tell me that they work jobs that they hate – just for the money – and that they're afraid to leave those jobs to pursue their own dreams and purpose because of their obligations and responsibilities to their families.

There are others who experience an empty void in their lives and who innately believe that there must be more to living than what they're currently doing, but they don't know what – nor how – to discover what it is.

I always recommend that people searching for their purpose begin by separating themselves from the negative voices in their heads – and that disconnecting from the media onslaught that attempts to get inside it will help. Spending quality time with yourself isn't a luxury, it's a necessity. Traditional meditation can be an effective tool for doing this, though it may not appeal to everyone.

There are also many other non-traditional types of meditation that I've used quite effectively. People who have long drives to work can use that time to get in touch with their inner voices. Chances are good that many already do this, even though some might consider it as nothing more than idle thinking or navel gazing. However, you can convert this to productive thinking – and gentle music can be great for doing this because it'll allow your mind to wander, and wandering thoughts can act as a net for catching ideas.

You can certainly use other methods. I still use my time on my treadmill or stationary bike as a catalyst for productive thinking. For me, the pairing of music through headphones and the resultant release of aerobic endorphins serve as a catalyst for generating some of my best thoughts and ideas.

Once you can silence some of the voices in your head, you might be surprised to actually hear your own inner voice – and this is when the fun begins. The good news is that there *is* a recipe of success for this, as Jerry would always point out.

I recommend finding a mentor or group of people with common interests to begin this process – you don't have to feel alone in this. You may find that as you move forward in these pursuits, you might reap more benefit from changing mentors – the way you change teachers in school as you progress through your education.

Once you have a grasp of your true purpose – even if it takes months or years until you fully implement your vision – you might discover that mentoring others becomes easier. You might realize that your employees struggle with issues that you've already learned about, similar to the way an eighth grader can easily understand a fifth grader's math studies and therefore, help them.

I often meet people who think they have to accomplish great feats or go halfway around the world to make some kind of difference in it. But the reality is that your greatest contribution could be to mentor others – right in your own backyard. This is why some of the best minds are in the teaching profession, despite what the media tells us.

I've met leaders who were afraid to mentor their subordinates for fear that those subordinates would leave the department or company. Not only is this shortsighted, from a business perspective, it's also morally wrong. There's no reason why you shouldn't always give your best to everyone every day. You just may be the one who inspires someone who will be the one to solve one of society's greatest challenges.

The most important thing to remember is that life is a journey. Don't let time's passing frighten you or lead you to believe that it's too late to do what you're here to do. One person may work at a company for 20 years before they become its CEO while another person may need 20 years of life experience to finally have the emotional capacity and depth to do what they're here to do. We are all on different paths and timelines.

I look forward to the day our paths cross as we go along on our life journeys.

Monica on love

Love. It's a word that's taken on many meanings for me in the years since I first met Joe. It certainly feels to me as if there is less love in the world at this moment than at any other time in history. It's as if global access to social media allows humanity to feed upon itself with every negative emotion available and that the more technological society becomes, the less humane it also becomes.

I'm still the manager of the same soup kitchen I worked at when I met Joe. Things have unfortunately gotten worse in the years since then. We're at a terrible point in our society. Changes in customer demographics at the kitchen have been dramatic and what was once a place that helped a few unfortunate souls who had no one to care for them is now a necessary destination for entire families in order to survive.

You would think that Love is probably the easiest of the Beans to incorporate into your life. I mean, who hasn't loved someone at some point in time? The Bean of Love actually represents more than what you'd consider typical love for another – it's a transcendent type of love; a love of beings, if you will.

Sometimes when I'm out shopping or running errands, I sadly observe someone treating their pet with more love than they would a stranger they might interact with. And occasionally, it's their children who receive less love.

People ask how you can go about incorporating this type of love. My answer is that love is about feelings. When you can feel good about yourself, you'll typically feel good about others. This is much easier to do if you're living your purpose.

It's difficult to be a great leader if you're in a job or occupation that feels wrong or not in alignment with your purpose. You'll always experience internal conflicts that will eventually lead to external conflicts because it's hard to keep those feelings hidden indefinitely. This profile fits the leader with poor engagement skills – the person that no one wants to work for. On the other hand, you flourish when you work in an occupation that you resonate with and love.

Loving another being means getting past their body and loving their soul – which you can access through your eyes. This is the great equalizer in life. How interesting this world would be if all we saw of each other were our eyes. Imagine if there were a huge screen blocking our views of each other's bodies. All of the things that color our impressions of others would be removed. How would that make you feel?

Imagine being overweight but knowing that the extra pounds couldn't be seen. How would that change your self-esteem? Or imagine yourself no longer being the wrong color when you go on a job interview. How would that affect your confidence? Or imagine if you had a disfigured face and when you met others, they couldn't see it. This is why some people love the anonymity of the internet – they feel good knowing that they can't be seen.

People who've experienced the Bean of Love view others as if there *were* a screen in front of them. There's no body to color their views of them. My guests at the soup kitchen could be wearing evening tuxedos and I wouldn't notice – because it's their eyes that I see.

Singh on tolerance

Assessing an event or period in your life is difficult until you have the benefit of time and distance, which adds perspective. I believed the world was in a dangerous situation when I first met Joe on his journey, as he not-so-eloquently let me know. Now that several years have passed, I look back at that time, fondly, as the good old days.

The world seems to have become not just more dangerous, but also unhappier. The number of people who spew hatred and venom seems to increase each day. I believe part of this is due to the anonymity of the internet where one can sit behind a keyboard – or be on a cell phone – and blog or comment for spiteful ends using social media.

It makes sense that if a person engages in venomous behavior all day, they'll assimilate that behavior into their personality, just as a person who is kind and caring, and who dedicates time to being helpful and generous towards others would naturally tend toward benevolent behavior.

Media today maintains a constant focus on polarizing politics and banal entertainment shows and profiles of celebrities. This continuous onslaught is mostly empty, the likes of which we've not seen before – but that we unfortunately and willingly embrace.

The Beans of Wisdom include the Bean of tolerance because it's an integral ingredient in dealing with all other beings in the world. It's not meant to embody so-called political correctness. People can say and do all 'the right things,' but I see the truth – and terror – in their eyes when, for example, I walk down the aisle of an airplane to my seat.

Tolerance is an attribute that truly great leaders share. It allows people to accept others' opinions in the workplace and acknowledge that there may be differing views on every topic.

I'm often asked how someone can acquire tolerance or, at the very least, become more tolerant than they are. The answer is quite simple, just as it is for all of the Beans. Pay attention to what you do in every moment – if you tend to react rather than respond to changes around you. By being present in the moment, you'll be more apt to acquire the desired behavior until it becomes instinctual.

I say it's simple and, of course, recognizing your own behavior is the difficult part. You have to control your responses to your thoughts and quiet the negative voices in your head – including those that come from outside of you – from media overload. Once you can silence the madness, a completely different world that you never noticed before can become available.

I recommend starting small, with just you. People commonly think that problems regarding tolerance involve big issues, but smaller, daily kinds of issues also hinge on varying levels of tolerance or lack of tolerance. Pay attention to how much tolerance you're able to muster as you drive in traffic or wait in a line – little things that drive you crazy, like when someone cuts in front of you – on the road or in a line – often have the effect of destroying your patience and with it, your ability to act with tolerance.

You might ask yourself how much tolerance you have with your co-workers' idiosyncrasies and personality differences. Maybe, more importantly, you could ask yourself what kind of tolerance you have for yourself and for your own quirks or habits. Are you tolerant of your own failures and shortcomings or do you beat yourself up every time you eat fattening food and fall off your diet?

Once you can view the world from this perspective, so many more things are possible.

Lucas on forgiveness

My life's taken quite a few turns since I met Joe that Christmas Eve some years ago. I moved out of town, so I no longer participate in the Beans of Wisdom, but it was a great experience for me while I participated. I still have affection for the days I spent in the white room! Since that time, I've learned that forgiveness is sometimes not as easy as I may have made it out to be that day.

The Bean of Forgiveness is about accepting responsibility for your own life, because each one of us creates what it is and where it can go. It was an easy concept for me to understand when I met Joe – since at that moment things were going well for me.

I've made my share of mistakes on the way to discovering that the world can be an unforgiving place for a young man covered in tattoos. As my friend Singh once pointed out, tolerance is in short supply in this world. After so much time of being treated like a criminal by so many people, it ended up becoming a self-fulfilling prophecy.

It unnerves me to speak about leadership since I don't believe I've ever been a great leader in my life, although I still have faith that one day I'll surprise my parents and make them proud.

I often speak to folks who are incarcerated on the topic of forgiveness and taking responsibility for your own life. At first, it was difficult because of the composition of the group, but then a strange thing began to happen. I noticed that the people on the inside were no different from the people on the outside – it's just that they had four walls surrounding them that kept them in.

It is *so* easy to blame others for our downfalls and shortcomings, and I guess that's why so many people do it. It took me a long time to accept responsibility for my own current situation, too – failure is never easy. Imagine my sticky situation of trying to convince people on the inside that they're where they are because of some bad decisions *they* made. It's a tough crowd, but I actually enjoy the challenge!

The more disturbing thing though, is that people on the outside live in their own types of prisons. They tend to accept mediocrity in their lives because they have to or they think they have to. For someone to be accountable for their own success in life, they also have to take responsibility for their failures, and that's something many people just can't overcome. It's close to impossible to rise out of the ashes like the Phoenix when you're filled with rage and negative energy. You almost feel like you have permission to fail.

People who really *do* want to change sometimes ask me how to go about cultivating forgiveness. Yes, I realize that there are professionals who address this sort of thing, and I even recommend them. But I also try to remember what I learned from Kris – that we have to forgive ourselves before we can begin forgiving others.

Great leaders know about the power of forgiveness because they've forgiven themselves many times for mistakes they made to finally get to where they are. Forgiving employees is powerful because it addresses the behavior and not the person. It's like granting someone a do-over or a second chance – and we all need one of those once in awhile.

Emma on compassion

Things haven't changed much for me over the last several years since I met Joe. I'm still a masseuse with a single massage table in one location, although a few times I've been offered the opportunity to open multiple locations. I've always turned down the offers because I don't think of myself as a businesswoman, but instead, as a kind of spiritual medium who's more concerned with transformation than money.

What I love about giving massages is the personal contact I make with my clients. I see what a massage does for a person – as Joe himself discovered in our initial meeting. It relieves the stress in their exhausted muscles, and even better, from their fatigued minds.

I still participate in the Beans of Wisdom event with Joe, but it's not the same since some of the people I loved there moved on, though I still feel great joy when I see the smiles on the children's faces. Once in awhile I get to meet up with one of the children after they've grown up. I treasure that!

We're living during a challenging time in the world – true compassion seems rare these days. But how can we be surprised? So much communication is no longer face-to-face for the most part, but instead, through text messages and email. It's hard to truly feel compassionate upon receiving important news by text message. Yet, that's where we are.

The great thing about having compassion is that it allows you to be present in the moment, not only with one person, but with whatever situation is going on at the time. Maybe you've experienced this for yourself – watching a sunset or a sunrise that was so breathtaking that you couldn't find the words to adequately describe it. You just watched it in silent awe and bathed in its beauty for those brief seconds, completely aware afterwards that you'd been part of something special.

These are the moments that begin to occur with more regularity as you eliminate the white noise in your head – kind of like the way you tune in on a radio frequency to hear something that catches your attention. Your focus becomes sharper and you'll begin to notice things you hadn't noticed before. You'll notice that living takes on a certain depth that you'd only experienced on rare occasions.

Great leaders who demonstrate the Bean of Compassion do this almost entirely without realizing it since it just becomes part of who they are – their authenticity. These people are the leaders that everyone wants to work for – as if they have a certain charisma about them that's magnetic.

It's been shown that compassion is something that leaders can develop with dedicated practice. It just requires that you focus your mind and observe your actions and responses with resolution – and then perform a brief self-analysis afterward to check that your attention didn't wander. Every interaction with an employee allows you the opportunity to assess your behavior and adjust it or change it as necessary, depending on the situation.

The analysis might seem awkward or unnatural at first, but after awhile you'll reach a point where you don't even have to think about it and it will just happen. Perhaps you've encountered a time when one of your associates wanted a day off for something important to them, but since you knew it was your busiest day you immediately just said 'no' without even considering it. How did that affect your associate's morale? What if you said 'yes' or at least considered it the next time? Do you think you could find a way to make it work? Think about what that would mean to your associate – and to your team.

Jerry on faith

This is a very complicated time in the world for having faith. I thought it was difficult when I first met Boss, but now it feels as if everywhere I turn there's cynicism and despair.

I think the world is still filled with hope, though – I mean, hope that someone will come along and fix our problems. Somehow I don't believe that there's a white knight or something out there in the world that'll come along to save us. No, I'm pretty sure that it's something that we – each one of us – will have to do for ourselves. Are you up to the task?

I've continued working with Joe since the first day we met. In fact, we've become good friends, getting together for good family times. It's been great to watch his boys grow up and see his family thrive after coming from the situation they were in some years ago.

I want to make it clear that Joe's latest success was wholly based on faith in his talents, his decisions and his team. He's no longer a man who sits around hoping and waiting for success and good times to arrive – he works to make it happen.

Boss doesn't just hope that his boys will grow into fine young men – he plants and cultivates his insights as if they were seeds of wisdom – and he explains the recipe for success to his boys. That makes it much easier for him to have faith that those seeds will yield strong roots.

The word 'faith' is often thrown around, especially in religious contexts. I never understood how a word such as *faith* could lead to the kinds of atrocities we see in the world today. It's apparent that we've learned very little as a civilization.

That being said, the Bean of Faith is not about dogma, but instead, about your belief in yourself. I believe we've arrived at a point in time where personal transformation is rapidly taking place on a global level. I think that so many people feel a sort of divine discontent and therefore, they're attempting to discover their true purpose in life – because they know there must be more. Can you feel it too?

Kris has spoken eloquently about how a person can discover their purpose and which steps to take to realize it. Faith is an integral part of that process. Sometimes faith is all we have to get us through the tough times.

This is something great leaders know about and experience on a daily basis. We sometimes forget that leaders must often make tough or unpopular decisions and have nothing to hang onto except for their belief in their decisions.

Critical thinking skills among employees are in short supply in this cookie-cutter business environment of ours today. This is one of the most important concepts that a leader can convey to his team. By teaching employees how to use and develop their critical thinking abilities – and have faith in their decisions – the leader builds capacity in the team and within each individual.

This is where a great leader excels – in having faith, not just in the decisions they make, but also in their associates' decisions. I think this is why Joe is such a successful father – he trusts in his sons and the decisions they'll make now and in the future.

Boss and I still get together occasionally to bake cupcakes for fun and to reminisce about when we first met. I still haven't learned to like vanilla frosting.

JJ on perseverance

I haven't seen much of Joe since that last day I met him, although I hear he's done amazing things since taking over for Kris. I was offered a position to work with aspiring paralympians and there was no way I could pass it up. Getting an opportunity like this to help athletes realize their dreams after they believed they were destroyed was the perfect challenge for me.

The Bean of Perseverance is the last Bean we give because everything else has to be in place before it. Perseverance is the glue to your dreams. All your talent, passion and vision mean nothing – if you give up and stop trying. If you do that, you relegate your dream to the graveyard where you'll find millions of other dreamers and the dreams they gave up on.

I won't bore you with the names of famous and not-so-famous people who've made some of the greatest discoveries of the last century or so. Think about it –so many things we take for granted every day wouldn't exist if they'd given up at some point in their journey.

The same can be said about many of the great businesses and products in the world today. Every technological device you use, everything you drive, everything you eat – all these things started as someone's visionary idea.

I'm often asked 'how much is enough'? When should I finally stop and give up and just resign myself to failure? But think about it – there's no such thing as enough – because you never know where or when a breakthrough will occur. As long as you keep trying, you haven't yet failed. How many times have you heard about someone getting his or her "big break"? That's nothing more than perseverance – keeping at it and then having fortuitous circumstances reveal themselves.

The key to the big break is staying "in the game." As long as you're in, you're open to the possibility of success. Sometimes you have to stay in the game through necessity while you gain the necessary wisdom to achieve your dream. It's okay to be a "late bloomer" – some people don't achieve their greatest success until they're older.

And some work for years at a company or career before they become a top player. The same can be said for rising through the ranks of the military. How come that's not seen as failure? Why would someone stay at a job or career for 10 or 20 years in order to progress at indeterminate intervals? Is that perseverance?

Once you have a vision of what you want to do, that's when the negative voices that say you're crazy and foolish begin. The negative chatter says 'you're not good enough' or 'who do you think you are?' Those are the same voices I heard when I trained for my Olympic medal. The voices said I was a long-shot medalist with two legs – so how on earth could I accomplish it with none?

The key will always be to listen to your inner voice. Sometimes the dream changes or atrophies and it's time for a new dream. You'll know when the time is right.

Author's profile

Copyright: Narro Photography

Joe Swinger is President of Wisdom Communications and Founder of High Definition Academy. He has gone from being homeless to a leader in multiple Fortune 500 companies where he has developed hundreds of successful business leaders while achieving extraordinary results. Joe speaks on a variety of topics, including leadership and personal development. He holds a Masters degree in both Psychology and Business Administration and currently lives in Albuquerque, NM. Joe may be contacted at joe@beansofwisdom.com